KT-558-546

1000 things you should know about

insects

C153123227

1000 things you should know about

insects

Edited by Barbara Taylor

Miles Kelly PUBLISHING

This material was first published as hardback in 2005

This edition published in 2006 by Miles Kelly Publishing Ltd
Bardfield Centre, Great Bardfield, Essex, CM7 4SL

Copyright © Miles Kelly Publishing Ltd 2006

2 4 6 8 10 9 7 5 3 1

Editorial Director: Belinda Gallagher
Art Director: Jo Brewer
Editor: Rosalind McGuire
Volume Designer: Ian Paulyn
Additional Design: Candice Bekir
Picture Researcher: Liberty Newton
Reprographics: Anthony Cambray, Mike Coupe,
Stephan Davis, Ian Paulyn

All rights reserved. No part of this publication may be reproduced,
stored in a retrieval system, or transmitted by any means, electronic,
mechanical, photocopying, recording or otherwise, without the prior
permission of the copyright holder.

British Library Cataloguing-in-Publication Data
A catalogue record for this book is available from the British Library

ISBN 1-84236-696-3

Printed in China

info@mileskelly.net
www.mileskelly.net

All artworks from the MKP Archives

All other photographs from:
Castrol, CMCD, Corbis, Corel, digitalSTOCK, digitalvision, Flat Earth,
Hemera, ILN, John Foxx, PhotoAlto, PhotoDisc, PhotoEssentials,
PhotoPro, Stockbyte

KENT
LIBRARIES & ARCHIVES
C153123227

CONTENTS

INSECT WORLD 6–12

ANTS, BEES AND WASPS 13–23

BUTTERFLIES AND MOTHS 23–34

FLIES, BEETLES AND BUGS 34–48

COCKROACHES, CRICKETS AND GRASSHOPPERS 49–55

OTHER INSECTS 56–61

Evolution

- **Insects are small animals** that belong to a class called Insecta. They are part of the phylum (group) called Arthropoda.

- **Arthropods** include crustaceans (crabs and their relatives), myriapods (centipedes and millipedes), and arachnids (spiders, mites and scorpions), as well as insects.

- **Some whole insects** were trapped and fossilized in amber (pine tree resin).

- **Some species of insects,** such as dragonflies or stoneflies, are so successful at surviving that they have not changed much over millions of years.

- **Entomologists have divided** all the insects discovered so far into 32 groups or orders.

- **The study of insects** is known as entomology.

◀ Trapped in sticky tree resin millions of years ago, this delicate insect was beautifully preserved as the soft resin turned into hard amber.

- **New species of insects** are constantly evolving as insects adapt themselves to their living conditions.

- **Fossils of insects** are sometimes preserved in rocks. These fossils are often only fragments of various insect body parts.

- **It is difficult to find** insect fossils because the soft bodies of insects decay quickly and do not become fossilized.

- **The oldest fossils** of tiny wingless insects were found to be 380 million years old.

Insect fact file

- **There are over one million** different species of insects, compared to just one human species.

- **Insects are successful survivors** because of their powerful exoskeletons, their ability to fly and their minute size.

- **Some insects can fly** for long distances. Some butterflies migrate thousands of kilometres to avoid bad weather.

- **Cockroaches have been living on Earth** for around 300 million years. Today's cockroaches look very similar to those living hundreds of millions of years ago.

- **Insects serve** as the largest source of food for other animals.

- **Fairyflies are the smallest insects** in the world. They are only 0.2 mm – about the size of a full stop.

- **Scientists have discovered the fossils** of a dragonfly that lived around 300 million years ago. Its wingspan was as big as a seagull.

◀ Moths and butterflies, such as this swallowtail butterfly, together make up one of the largest groups of insects. There are ten times more moths than butterflies.

- **People have domesticated silkworms** for so long that these insects do not exist in the wild anymore.

- **Insects are cold-blooded animals,** so their growth and development depends upon how hot or cold the weather is.

- **Scientists have developed 'insect robots'** that copy the agility of real insects. These robots are used to explore dangerous areas, such as minefields and the surface of other planets. Robots are not nearly as agile as real insects, but mimic the way they move.

Insect firsts

● **Insects made the first paper!** Paper wasps chew the bark of some plants and add saliva to make a type of paper. This 'paper' is used for building nests.

● **Insects such as the dragonfly** were the first ever fliers on Earth.

● **Insects were the first animals** to use sound to communicate. Bees use buzzing sounds to warn about danger, indicate the presence of food and convey various other types of information.

● **Cicadas and crickets** have been captured and reared by humans for the beautiful sound they make.

● **Dragonflies are known to hover**, like modern day helicopters, over their prey.

> ★ **STAR FACT** ★
> Insects were the first doctors! Some insects produce toxins to combat and treat infections and diseases that occur in their bodies.

▶ *Butterflies were among the first pollinating insects.*

● **Termites made the first ever colonies** where the inhabitants all had different jobs. There are queens, soldiers and workers in termite colonies.

● **Insects were the first to** 'tame' other animals. Ants 'tame' the larvae of some butterflies and aphids and extract a type of sugary liquid called honeydew from them.

● **Dragonflies invented** 'fast food' long before humans! They hold prey with their legs and eat while flying.

● **Insects used the techniques of camouflage** and ambush for defence and attack long before humans used them in military operations.

Insects and people

▶ *People began to domesticate bees about 3000 years ago. Today, most domesticated honeybees are kept in beehives containing removable frames. The bees store honey in the upper frames, which the beekeeper removes to harvest the honey.*

● **Insects were always** of great importance to human civilizations. People rear insects such as silkworms and honeybees to obtain important materials from them, such as silk, honey and wax.

● **Archaeologists have discovered** prehistoric cave paintings that show scenes of honey collection and the extraction of honey from beehives.

● **Many insects,** such as mosquitoes and bed bugs, feed on human blood.

● **Japanese Samurai warriors** painted intricate butterfly patterns on weapons and flags to symbolize nobility.

● **Many stories, songs and poems** have been written about different insects in different cultures of the world.

● **Many people eat insects** such as termites, cicadas and leafcutter ants, and consider them to be delicacies.

● **Deadly diseases** such as the Bubonic plague were transmitted to humans from tiny insects such as fleas, and caused millions of deaths.

● **Doctors used to insert maggots** in wounds to eat dead flesh and disinfect the wounds by killing bacteria.

● **Many insects feed on agricultural pests** and help farmers.

● **Some insects can be pests** and can destroy crops and fields and cause serious damage.

Sacred insects

▶ Images of scarab beetles were often carved on ancient Egyptian precious stones and jewellery. The carvings were thought to bring luck and ward off evil.

● **Ancient Egyptians worshipped** an array of beetles and other creepy crawlies, such as centipedes and scorpions.

● **The scarab or the dung beetle** was associated with the creator-god, Atum. This beetle was believed to have come into being by itself, from a ball of dung.

● **The wings of the jewel bug** are metallic green, purple and golden in colour. It is another insect revered by the ancient Egyptians.

● **Egyptians used amulets** with motifs of insects, such as locusts, beetles and flies, for good luck.

● **Egyptians believed that honey** could protect them from evil spirits.

● **Motifs of butterflies** have been discovered on ancient tombs and jewellery.

● **Some Moslems believe** that a praying mantis in the praying posture offers prayers towards Mecca.

● **Tiny black ants** are revered by some Hindus in India.

● **The ancient Chinese** regarded cicadas as a symbol of immortality and rebirth.

★ STAR FACT ★
Honeybees were believed to be the tears of the Egyptian Sun-god, Ra.

Anatomy

● **The segmented body** of an insect is divided into three parts: head, thorax (middle section) and abdomen (rear section).

● **All insects have six legs** that are joined to the thorax. They usually have either one or two pairs of wings, which are also joined to the thorax.

● **All nsects have an exoskeleton** – a strong outer skeleton that protects the insect's body.

● **The muscles and delicate organs** of insects are enclosed and protected within this exoskeleton.

● **All insects have two antennae** on their head. These are used to sense smell, touch and sound.

● **The head also contains** mouthparts that are adapted to different feeding methods, such as chewing, biting, stabbing and sucking.

Antenna
Compound eye
Head
Thorax
Wing
Leg
Abdomen

◀ This diagram of a honeybee shows the main parts of an insect's body. A honeybee has two pairs of wings.

● **The digestive and reproductive systems** of insects are contained in the abdomen.

● **Insects have an open circulatory system** without lots of tubes for carrying blood. The heart of an insect is a simple tube that pumps greenish-yellow blood all over the body.

● **Insects breathe** through special openings on the side of the body called spiracles.

● **Insects have tiny brains,** which are just collections of nerve cells fused together. The brain sends signals to control all the other organs in the body.

Moulting

- **Moulting is the shedding of the hard exoskeleton** periodically because it does not stretch as the insect grows bigger. All insects moult during the early stages of their life.

- **Insects swallow air** or water or use blood pressure to expand their body, causing the exoskeleton to split.

- **A soft new exoskeleton** is exposed when the insect gets rid of its old one. The new exoskeleton is bigger in size and allows the insect to expand.

- **The new exoskeleton hardens** and becomes darker in colour.

- **Insects normally moult** five to ten times in a lifetime.

> ★ STAR FACT ★
> A caterpillar grows about 2000 times bigger than its size at the time of its birth. If a 3 kg human baby grew at the same rate, the baby would weigh as much as a bus in a month.

▶ A young adult dragonfly emerges during its moult. After resting, it will pump blood into its short wings to spread them out to their full adult size.

- **A silverfish** can moult up to 60 times in a lifetime.

- **The larval stage** between moults is known as an instar.

- **Moulting takes a long time** and the insect is vulnerable to predatory attacks during this period. Most insects moult in secluded areas.

- **Other animals,** such as snakes and spiders, also moult in order to grow.

Defence

- **As well as camouflage** and mimicry, insects also use other strategies to protect themselves from predators.

- **Some caterpillars and larvae** have special glands that secrete poison when they are attacked. Predatory birds soon learn to avoid them.

- **Ants, bees and wasps** can deliver stings to an attacker. These insects pump in venom and cause pain and irritation.

- **Stick insects and weevils** are known to 'play dead' when attacked. They keep very still and the attacker leaves the insects alone because most predators do not eat dead prey.

- **Some butterflies,** such as the monarch butterfly, are poisonous and cause the attacking bird to vomit if it eats the butterfly.

- **Some insects, such as katydids,** shed limbs if an attacker grabs them by the leg. This process is known as autotomy.

◀ This katydid could escape from the formidable claws of a desert scorpion by shedding a leg and flying away.

- **The bombardier beetle** has special glands, which enable it to spray boiling hot poisonous fluids at an attacker.

- **Moths, grasshoppers and mantids** show the bright colours on their hind wings to startle a predator. These are called flash colours.

- **Stink glands** present in some bugs release obnoxious and repelling smells that predators cannot tolerate.

- **When alarmed,** ants raise their abdomen. This sends a signal to other ants in the colony, and all the other ants raise their abdomens too.

Camouflage and mimicry

● **Insects use defence strategies**, such as camouflage and mimicry, to protect themselves from predators. Killer insects sometimes use the same strategies to catch their prey.

● **Some insects cleverly hide themselves** by blending in with their surroundings. This is known as camouflage.

● **Some harmless insects** mimic (imitate) harmful insects in appearance and behaviour to fool predators into leaving them alone.

● **Hoverflies have yellow-and-black stripes** on their bodies, which makes them resemble stinging insects such as wasps or hornets. so predators avoid them.

● **The larvae of some butterflies** resemble bird droppings, or even soil.

● **Some moths imitate dangerous wasps and bees** in behaviour and sound. Their buzz startles predators.

● **Stick insects** and praying mantids appear to be the twigs and leaves of plants.They blend into their environment so well that they are often missed by predators.

▶ The hornet moth has a yellow-and-black striped body, making it look like a large wasp called a hornet. It even behaves like a hornet. Predators avoid hornet moths because they look as if they might sting.

● **Monarch butterflies** are bitter-tasting and poisonous, so birds do not eat them. Viceroy butterflies have orange and black wings similar to those of monarch butterflies. Birds avoid viceroy butterflies because they think that they are poisonous as well.

● **Adults and caterpillars** of some moths and butterflies have large eyelike spots to scare away predatory birds.

● **The velvet ant** is actually a wasp. It resembles an ant and can easily attack ant nests with this disguise.

Hornet

Hornet moth

Stings

● **Insects that belong** to the Hymenopteran order, such as ants, bees and wasps, are the most familiar stinging insects.

● **A stinging insect** has special organs that secrete venom (poison) and a sharp sting or teeth to inject venom into the victim.

● **The venom** can have a paralyzing effect on the prey. It can also damage tissues and cause pain. Hornet venom is the most potent.

● **Insect venom consists of** enzymes, proteins and chemicals known as alkaloids.

● **Some insects,** such as mosquitoes, do not sting. They puncture the skin surface in order to suck up blood. Such insects can spread various diseases, such as malaria.

● **Insects sting** for two purposes – to catch prey and to defend themselves from predators.

◀ A honeybee's jagged sting is a modified egg-laying tool, so only female bees can sting. Male bees do not have the necessary equipment.

● **Honeybees sting only once** and die soon after that. Their jagged stings remain stuck in their victim's skin, which tears out the honeybee's insides.

● **Wasps sting their victims** many times over because their stings are smooth and can be pulled out of the victims and used again.

● **Ants normally sting** as well as bite. They inject formic acid when they sting.

★ STAR FACT ★
Ant venom glands have evolved to produce a chemical called pheromones, which the ants use to communicate.

Habitats

● **Insects have adapted themselves** to survive in almost every habitat on Earth, including some with extreme climates.

● **Entomologists have discovered** certain species of insect that live on volcanic lava and others that survive in cold polar regions.

● **Most insects live in** tropical regions where the warm temperatures are most suitable for their growth and development.

● **Insects can live** in the freshwater of ponds, lakes, streams, rivers, and even muddy pools and small waterholes.

● **Some insect species** can live very deep underwater while others need to come to the surface to breathe in air.

● **Many insects lay their eggs** in water and their larvae thrive underwater. These insects fly out to live in the air when they become adults.

● **The larvae of house-flies** grow up in animal manure and household waste.

● **Some insects can survive** on the surface of ponds of crude oil. They feed on other insects that fall into the oil.

● **Some insects can survive** on man-made food sources, such as glue, paint, clothes and paper. They make their homes in our homes.

> ★ **STAR FACT** ★
> Around 97 percent of the insect world lives on the land or in freshwater. Very few insects can survive in the sea.

▼ Temperate woodlands are home to a rich variety of insects because of the range of food and shelter available. The numbers and species of insect living in woodlands vary with the seasons and the types of trees dominating the woodlands.

Key

1 Elm beetle

2 Furniture beetle

3 Flower bug

4 Shield bug

Winter survival

- **Insects use various methods** to survive cold winters. Many go into a deep sleep called hibernation. Their body temperature falls to just above that of the surroundings and vital body processes slow down.

- **Some insects go into a dormant state** called diapause. They stop developing and growing. Diapause is most common among moth pupae.

- **Some insects spend winter** in swellings (galls), that they cause on plants. Galls provide these insects with food and shelter.

- **Beetles and ants** may burrow deep furrows in the ground and keep themselves warm inside them.

- **Ladybirds cluster together** in huge numbers when they hibernate.

- **Some species of beetle** store fat in their bodies to keep themselves warm.

◀ Many insects find safe places in which to survive the winter. Peacock butterflies have a chemical 'antifreeze' that helps to stop their body fluids freezing during cold weather.

- **Some butterflies and moths** survive the winter by hibernating in tree holes or caves. They may hibernate for months before emerging in spring or summer.

- **Some insects survive** the winter as eggs, which only start to develop the following spring.

- **Some insects replace the water content** in their body with glycerol, which works as an antifreeze.

- **Honeybees stay inside their hives** during cold weather. They vibrate their wings or cluster together to keep warm.

Migration

- **Insects migrate** great distances in search of suitable living and breeding conditions. They often migrate when the weather changes or when food becomes scarce.

- **Migrating insects** may land in some places and lay a large number of eggs before moving on.

- **Insects migrate in two ways**, which are known as homeostatic and dynamic migration.

- **Homeostatic migration** is when insects pass through a defined path and return the same way. In dynamic migration, insects use the wind or tides to decide their path.

- **Monarch butterflies** migrate across continents, covering a distance of more than 3000 km.

- **Pilots have spotted** migrating butterflies at an altitude of 1200 m.

★ **STAR FACT** ★
Migrating butterflies such as the painted lady do not return to their home ground, but the next generation does.

- **Butterflies sometimes travel** in huge groups. Most of the older butterflies cannot withstand the journey and die on the way.

- **Locusts migrate across farmlands** in large swarms in their search for greener pastures.

- **Army ants** do not build permanent nests because they constantly migrate in search of food.

◀ Every autumn, monarch butterflies fly from the northern areas of North America to the warmth of Florida, California and Mexico. In spring, new generations of monarchs make the long return journey north again.

Ants

● **Ants are one of the most** successful insects on Earth. There are more than 9000 different species.

● **The study of ants** is known as myrmecology. People sometimes rear ants in elaborate ant farms.

● **Ants belong to an order of insects** known as Hymenoptera. Bees and wasps also belong to this group.

● **Entomologists believe** that ants evolved from wasps millions of years ago.

● **Ants are social insects** and live in huge colonies. These colonies consist of the queen ant, female workers and male ants.

● **An ant can lift a weight** that is 20 to 50 times more than its own body weight.

▶ *When ants find food, they form a chemical trail of pheromones so that other ants can find their way from the nest to the food source.*

● **In ant colonies,** the different ants divide themselves into groups that perform various tasks. Some ants are cleaners, some take care of the young while others gather food or defend the nest.

● **Ants are intelligent.** Experts have discovered that ant brains can function as fast as a powerful computer.

● **Ants spray formic acid** on predators as a form of defence. People used to obtain this acid by boiling ants.

★ **STAR FACT** ★
Birds allow ants to crawl on their bodies and spray them with formic acid. Known as anting, this gets rid of parasites from their feathers.

More ants

● **Most ants live in anthills** made of mounds of soil, sand and sticks, but some nest in trees.

● **Anthills consist** of different chambers and tunnels. Each chamber is used for different purposes, such as food storage, nurseries or resting areas.

◀ *Tailor, or weaver, ants make nests out of leaves or similar materials sewed together with silk produced by the larvae.*

● **Male ants** die shortly after mating with the queen ant.

● **Not all ants live in anthills.** Army ants are nomadic in nature. They carry their eggs and young with them while travelling and set up temporary camps.

● **The queen** is the largest ant in the colony. When she matures, she flies off to find a place to build a new colony.

● **Queen ants** nip off their wings once they find a place to breed. Smaller worker ants also have wings.

● **Worker ants** take care of the eggs. At night, they carry the eggs into deep nest tunnels for protection. In the morning, the workers carry the eggs back to the surface.

● **Ants have two stomachs.** One stomach carries its own food while the other carries food that will be shared with other ants. This is called the crop.

● **Ants communicate** with the help of their feelers (antennae). They also leave scent trails behind them to let the other ants know where exactly to find the food source.

● **Each ant colony** has a unique smell that helps the members to identify each other. This also helps the ants to detect an intruder in the nest.

Army ant

- **Army ants** constantly migrate in search of food. They can attack and enslave ants living in other colonies.

- **Army ants march only at night** and stop to camp in the morning.

- **Army ants are nomadic** in nature, and do not build permanent nests.

- **Temporary nests** are formed by army ants while the queen lays her eggs. The ants cling onto each other and form the walls and chambers.

- **Army ants are voracious eaters.** They march in swarms of up to one million ants and eat nearly 50,000 insects in a single day!

- **These ants eat insects,** birds and small animals that cross their path. Army ants can even eat a horse.

★ STAR FACT ★
A queen army ant can lay up to 4 million eggs in one month.

- **Army ants have simple** and not compound eyes like other ant species. However, worker army ants are blind.

- **Army ants have not evolved** (changed) much in the last 100 million years.

- **Some people allow army ants** to march into their homes and clear them of insects and other pests.

▼ The army ants of tropical America march in columns. To cross gaps, some of the ants form bridges with their bodies, allowing the rest of the army to swarm over them. The worker ants also link up to form chains that surround the queen and young.

Leafcutter ant

● **Leafcutter ants** cut out bits of leaves from plants and carry them back to their underground nest.

● **Leafcutter ants cannot digest** leaves. They feed on a fungus that is specially grown by them.

● **The cut leaf pieces** are used to fertilize fungus farms that are grown inside the ant nest. There can be several farms in a single nest.

● **A queen leafcutter ant** can produce about 15 million offspring during her lifetime.

● **Leafcutter ants divide themselves** into workers and soldiers. The soldiers are bigger, and they protect the nest.

● **Small worker ants** take care of the young and the nest, while the bigger worker ants collect pieces of leaves.

● **In some species of leafcutter ant,** tiny workers ride on the pieces of snipped leaves. They protect the larger workers from flies that try to lay their eggs on them.

● **Leafcutter ants are usually found** in tropical rainforests.

● **Leafcutter ants are eaten** in some cultures. They are a rich source of protein.

● **Leafcutter ants do not sting,** but they can bite.

◀ Leafcutter ants in Central and South American rainforests often cut leaves 50 to 200 m away from their nest. Each leaf fragment can take two or three minutes to cut and is many times bigger than the tiny ant.

Weaver ant

▶ Weaver ants joining leaves together to make their nest.

● **Weaver ants** build their colonies in the treetops, using live green leaves.

● **The larvae of weaver ants** secrete a sticky silklike substance. Adult ants use the larvae like glue sticks.

● **A team of adult worker weaver ants** holds two leaves together. Another worker holds the larva in its mandibles (mouthparts) and uses the silky secretion to stick the leaves together.

● **A colony can contain** about 150 weaver nests in 20 different trees. The queen ant's nest is built in the centre of the colony. It is made with extra silk and is feathery in appearance.

● **The larger worker** (soldier) ants protect the nest. Smaller workers take care of various chores inside the nest.

● **Weaver ants are carnivores** and feed on body fluids from small, soft bodied insects. Some species also feed on honeydew.

● **For 2000 years,** the Chinese have used weaver ants to control pests in their fields.

● **Weaver ants do not sting** but they can inflict very painful bites if provoked. When they bite, weaver ants squirt formic acid into the wound, which causes even more pain.

● **Some caterpillars and spiders** camouflage themselves as weaver ants and attack weaver ant nests. The spiders may even smell like weaver ants.

★ STAR FACT ★
Weaver ants are eaten in Eastern cultures. The oil extracted from these ants is often used as sweeteners in food.

Bees

- **There are approximately** 20,000 species of bee. Some live alone but over 500 species are social and live in colonies.

- **Bees are small** – only 2 to 4 cm in length. They have hairs and a sting to protect them. The hairs also help them to collect pollen.

- **Bees are usually black** or grey in colour but can also be yellow, red, green or blue.

- **Bees feed on pollen and nectar** from flowers. Pollen contains protein and nectar provides energy.

- **Social bees secrete wax** to build their nests. A honeybee colony may contain 3000 to 40,000 bees. It consists of a single queen bee, female workers and male drones.

- **The male drones do not have stings** and their function is to mate with the queen bee. The queen lays about 600 to 700 eggs every day.

◀ Honeybee workers crowd around their queen. The workers stroke and lick the queen to pick up scents called pheromones, which pass on information.

- **Bees have five eyes.** They have two compound eyes and three simple eyes, or ocelli. Bees cannot see red but they can see ultraviolet light, which is invisible to us.

- **A normal bee's lifespan** ranges from five to six weeks but a queen bee can live up to five years.

- **Bees communicate with other bees** about the distance, direction and quantity of the food source through a unique combination of dance and sounds.

- **A honeybee attacks** to protect itself or its colony. Once a bee stings, it leaves behind its sting and venom in the victim's body. As the bee pulls away from the victim, it dies when its organs are pulled out of its abdomen.

Bee behaviour

- **Bees have two kinds of mouthparts.** The first, found in honeybees, is adapted for sucking. The other is adapted for biting. This is found in carpenter bees.

- **The antennae are the organs** of touch and smell. Bees use them to detect flower fragrances and to find nectar.

- **Bees can rarely distinguish** sweet and bitter tastes but can identify sour and salty tastes. Bees use their front legs, antennae and proboscis for tasting.

- **Bees have no ears,** but they can sense vibrations through their sensitive hairs.

- **Bees do not sleep at night,** although they remain motionless.

- **Wild bees nest underground** or in tree holes, caves or under houses. Honeybees also live in hives constructed by people.

◀ Bees are important because they carry pollen from flower to flower so that seeds can grow.

- **Social bees** live in large colonies of queens, males and workers. Males do not help in the organization and other activities of the colony.

- **When a colony becomes overcrowded,** some of the bees fly to a new location. This is called swarming.

- **The queen bee lays eggs** and male bees fertilize the queen bee. Worker bees perform various tasks, such as cleaning the cells, keeping the young warm, feeding larvae and collecting food for the colony.

- **The queen bee secretes pheromones,** which inhibit the development of worker bees into queens. Once she lays eggs, the fertilized eggs become female worker bees and the unfertilized eggs become male bees.

Bee nests

- **Social bees make complex nests,** which consist of a number of cells, often built in flat sheets called combs.

- **Social bees** make cells of wax. However, honeybees are the only species that makes prominent honeycombs. People sometimes keep honeybees in hives for their honey.

- **Honeycombs** are divided into three sections. The upper section is used for storing honey, the middle section for storing pollen. The lower section holds eggs and young.

- **The hexagonal shape** of the honeycomb cells allows the maximum amount of honey to be stored using the least amount of wax.

- **Social bees use their nests** to raise their eggs, larvae and pupae – their brood. Some also use their nests to prepare and store honey for the winter.

- **Bees use 'bee glue'** (propolis), a sticky tree resin, to strengthen and repair their nests.

▶ A honeybee hive showing some of the cells used for storing pollen, honey eggs or developing larvae.

- **Bees use water** as a coolant to maintain an optimum temperature of $35°$ C in a beehive.

- **Male drones** have bigger cells than the female workers in a honeybee hive.

- **A bumblebee queen** builds her nest in a hole in the ground.

- **Stingless bees** build saclike combs made from a mixture of resin and wax called cerumen. The combs are held together by propolis in the hollows of trees, rocks and walls.

Honey

- **Honey** is a natural, unrefined sweetener, which is an alternative to sugar.

- **Every 100 g of honey** provides 319 kcal of energy.

- **Bees collect the nectar** of flowers, and other plant secretions, and turn it into honey. It is then altered chemically into different types of sugars and stored in the comb cells.

- **The honey in a honeycomb** includes matured nectar, pollen, bee saliva and wax granules.

- **Honey mainly contains** moisture, sugars and minerals. Several trace elements, such as calcium, phosphorous, magnesium, iron, silica and vitamin C, are also present.

- **Honey is considered** to be the only source of food that has all the energy and protein reserves necessary to sustain life.

◀ A natural honeycomb, showing the double layer of six-sided cells constructed by the bees to store honey. The honeycomb is used in the winter as food for the larvae and other members of the colony.

- **The colour and flavour of honey** depends upon the climate and the flowers from which the nectar has been collected.

- **Honey serves as an important source** of medicines because of its mild laxative, bactericidal, sedative, antiseptic and alkaline characteristics.

- **Honey extracted from wild beehives** can be dangerous if the nectar is obtained from poisonous flowers.

- **Honey is used in a fluid medium** in the preservation of the cornea (layer at the front of the eye).

Bumblebee

- **Bumblebees are hairy.** They are black, yellow or orange in colour and up to 25 mm long. They are most common in temperate regions.

- **Bumblebees live** in small colonies of between 50 to 600 bees.

- **Bumblebees build their nests** on the ground in grassy hollows or deserted nests. The chambers are spherical with one exit. The cells inside are capsule shaped.

◀ The bee combs the pollen from its body and packs it tightly into the pollen baskets (long, stiff bristles) on its back legs.

- **The queen bumblebee** lays her eggs in wax cups inside the nest. The wax is secreted by her abdominal glands.

- **Only the young queen bumblebees** survive the winter. The rest of the bees in the colony die.

- **Bumblebees regulate their body temperature** using their body hair. The queens hibernate in winter and emerge in the spring to lay eggs and start a new colony.

- **Bumblebees are low fliers** and move slowly around the flowers.

- **Bumblebees help to pollinate plants,** such as red clover. Their long tongue enables them to reach deep inside flowers.

> ★ STAR FACT ★
> Bumblebees do not produce large quantities of honey. They store honey just for feeding themselves and their young.

- **In summer,** the bumblebee workers fan their wings to cool the developing young. The buzzing sound of fanning is so loud that it can be heard from a distance.

Carpenter bee

- **Carpenter bees** are named after their habit of drilling into wood for building nests.

- **Blue-black or metallic in colour,** carpenter bees resemble large bumblebees.

- **Carpenter bees** are found all over the world, especially in areas where woody plants flourish. They are common in forested regions of the tropics.

- **Carpenter bees are solitary** in nature and do not live in colonies.

- **Male carpenter bees** have white-coloured faces or white markings and females have black-coloured faces.

- **Males do not have a sting** but they do guard the nest. The females do have stings but are very docile and do not sting unless in danger.

> ★ STAR FACT ★
> Adult carpenter bees hibernate during the winter. They remain in their wooden nest, surviving on stored honey and pollen.

◀ A carpenter bee is about 20 to 25 mm long. It is less hairy than a bumblebee, with short hairs on its abdomen or none at all.

- **Female carpenter bees** nest in their wooden tunnels. They prefer weathered, unpainted, bare wood. In these tunnels, carpenter bees drill holes, where they lay eggs in individual cells and store enough food for the larvae to grow. There is only a single entrance to each tunnel.

- **People take preventive measures,** such as spraying pesticides, to keep carpenter bees away from their home and gardens.

Honeybee

● **Honeybees are social insects.** They live in large colonies and are the most popular species of bees.

● **Some well-known species** of honeybee are Italian bees, Carniolan (Slovenian) bees, Caucasian bees, German black bees and Africanized honeybees.

● **In a honeybee colony,** different groups of bees carry out different tasks. A colony is made up of a queen bee, female workers and male drones.

● **Queen bees** are sexually productive and responsible for laying eggs that develop into drones and worker bees.

● **Worker bees** have a sharp sting, pollen baskets, wax secreting glands and a honey sac for collecting honey. The wax is used to build sheets of cells called combs.

● **Honeybees are the biggest producers of honey.** This is why they are the species most domesticated by humans.

◄ *Honeybees have a hairy thorax and an abdomen with orange-yellow rings separating the segments.*

● **Worker bees build the nest** as well as collect pollen and nectar for food. They are also responsible for maintaining the nursery temperature at 34°C, which is ideal for hatching the eggs and rearing the larvae.

● **Drones do not have a sting.** Their sole function is to mate with the queen, and they die after mating. During the winter, they are driven out by the workers to die.

● **Honeybees** have an amazing mode of communication among themselves – dancing. Dr Karl Von Frisch won the Nobel Prize for deciphering the bee dance.

● **Honeybees are susceptible** to various diseases and attacks by parasites. Parasite and virus attacks may cause paralysis in bees.

Leafcutter bee

● **Leafcutter bees are named** after their habit of cutting pieces of leaf to make a protective casing for their eggs. They nest in the soil or hollow plant stems.

● **They have hair** on their back, which helps them collect pollen.

● **Most leafcutter bees** are solitary, and females construct individual nests. Males are smaller than females and have hairy faces.

● **The female bee** builds her nest from leaf pieces. Once a cell is ready, she stores pollen and honey inside, lays an egg and closes the cell with a disk of leaf. Then she repeats the sequence until the entire nest is complete.

● **Individual female leafcutter bees** do all the work. They select the nesting place, construct cells, lay the eggs and rear the larvae.

● **Leafcutter bees are docile** with a mild sting. They use the sting to defend themselves.

◄ *A female leafcutter bee snips off a piece of leaf with her sharp jaws. She will roll up the leaf fragment and carry it between her legs as she flies back to her nest.*

● **It is possible** for leafcutter bees to harm plants because of their habit of constructing nests with plant leaves.

● **Leafcutter bees help some plants,** such as alfalfa, with pollination. They do this by carrying the pollen from one plant to another.

● **The predators of the leafcutter bee** include wasps, velvet ants and some species of blister beetle.

★ **STAR FACT** ★
The average lifespan of a female leafcutter bee is two months and in this time, she lays 30 to 40 eggs.

Wasps

▶ This close-up of a wasp's head shows the large black compound eyes, which are good at detecting movement and can see certain colours. Wasps also have sharp, cutting jaws with jagged edges.

● **Wasps belong to the Hymenopteran order,** as do bees and ants. They have hard exoskeletons and their bodies are divided into head, thorax and abdomen. They all have transparent wings and two compound eyes.

● **Wasps are solitary** as well as social insects. Social wasps live in huge colonies while solitary wasps live alone. There are about 17,000 species of wasps, but only about 1500 species are social.

● **Wasp nests can be simple or complex.** Some nests are just burrows in the ground while others are built with mud and twigs and can have many cells and tunnels.

★ STAR FACT ★
When disturbed, female wasps can sting.

● **Each nest has at least one queen wasp** as well as workers and males.

● **Not all wasps build nests.** Some wasps such as cuckoo wasps, lay eggs in the nests of other bees and other wasps.

● **Other species of wasp** lay their eggs in stems, leaves, fruits and flowers instead of building nests.

● **Adult wasps feed on nectar,** and fruit and plant sap while the larvae feed on insects.

● **Many species of wasp** are parasitic in nature, which means that they live part of their lives as parasites inside other insects. The larvae of such wasps feed on other insects and sometimes eat plant tissues.

● **Wasps are helpful for controlling pests,** such as caterpillars.

Hornet

● **Hornets belong to the order** Hymenoptera and the Vespidae family. They have dark brown and yellow stripes all over their body.

● **Hornets are known for their ferocious nature** and painful sting. They are huge, robust wasps and are social in nature.

● **Social hornets form huge colonies** that can contain about 25,000 individuals.

● **Hornets can build their nest anywhere** – at a height or even on the ground. They insulate their nests with layers of 'paper'.

● **These insects chew plant fibre** and mix it with saliva to form a papery paste, which they use to build nests. The nest is spherical, with an entrance at the bottom and is divided into many tiers inside. These tiers have hexagonal cells, in which the young ones are raised.

● **Hornets build the largest nests** of all wasps. A hornet nest can be 122 cm long and 91 cm in circumference.

▶ Hornets can be 30 mm in length. They can be distinguished from wasps by their larger size and deeper yellow colour.

● **Hornet colonies die out in one year.** No member of the colony survives the winter except the female hornets that have mated.

● **Abandoned hornet nests** provide shelter to other insects during the winter.

● **Some insects have stripes,** which resemble those of hornets. These ward off predators, which mistake harmless insects for hornets.

★ STAR FACT ★
Hornets are known to chase their tormentors.
Hence the saying 'never stir a hornet's nest'.

Gall wasp

● **Gall wasps are small parasitic insects** that feed on plants.

● **These insects are named** after their habit of causing the formation of a tumour-like growth in plants, known as galls.

● **Galls are an abnormal growth** of plant tissues and leaves. Some of them look like greenish apples or berries on leaves.

● **Galls are formed when** a female gall wasp injects her eggs into a plant. When the eggs hatch, the larvae release some chemicals, which causes the plant to cover them with soft tissues in the form of a gall.

● **Galls can be either** spongy or hollow inside.

● **Gall wasp larvae** feed on the gall and pupate inside it. Adult gall wasps emerge from the gall either by boring a hole or by bursting it through the surface.

◀ *Gall wasps are usually about 2 to 8 mm long. Their shiny abdomen is oval in shape and their*

● **Different types of galls,** such as leaf, flower, seed and stem galls, are caused by different species of gall wasp.

● **A gall is like a nursery** for one or more species of gall wasp.

● **A species of gall wasp,** known as a fig wasp, causes the formation of seed galls inside wild figs and in the process, pollinates them. No other insect pollinates wild figs.

● **Gall wasps are very selective** about the plants on which they lay their eggs. For instance, some gall wasps lay their eggs on figs, while others prefer roses.

▼ *Female fig wasps lay eggs on flowers inside immature figs. The eggs develop into larvae, pupae and adults. Adult females emerge and fly off to find other figs in which to lay their eggs. The wingless male wasps die without ever leaving the fig.*

Paper wasp

▶ The small nest entrance is easy to defend from other insects.

● **Paper wasps** are reddish-brown in colour and have yellow stripes on their body.

● **They are social insects** and live in small colonies of 20 to 30 insects. After the queen wasp mates, she builds a nest made of six-sided cells covered in layers of paper. The nests are mostly built in the spring.

● **Paper wasps chew plant fibre,** which they mix with their saliva to build their nests.

● **A few queen paper wasps** build a nest together. The most powerful queen dominates and leads the colony, while the others become workers.

● **Some paper wasp nests** look like inverted umbrellas, so these insects are also known as 'umbrella wasps'.

● **The subordinate queen wasps** are called joiners. Sometimes, a joiner manages to overpower the reigning queen. She becomes the new queen while the original queen becomes a worker.

● **Unlike other wasps,** bees and ants, queen paper wasps closely resemble the worker wasps.

● **Adult paper wasps** feed only on nectar while the young larvae feed on chewed insects.

● **Sometimes, army ants** invade paper wasp nests and destroy the entire colony.

> ★ STAR FACT ★
> The Chinese were inspired by the humble paper wasp to invent paper.

Parasitic wasps

● **Parasitic wasps lay their eggs** inside other wasps, spiders and insects, such as bees, caterpillars and aphids.

● **Female parasitic wasps** inject their eggs into the body of their host using an ovipositor (egg-laying tube). Once the eggs hatch, the larvae eat their way out of the host.

● **Parasitic wasps can lay as many as** 3000 eggs inside a single host insect.

● **Some parasitic wasps** are known for infesting moth and butterfly caterpillars. They are helpful for controlling the caterpillar populations in fields.

● **Some tiny wasps** specialize in parasitizing insect eggs. The eggs of these wasps can multiply into many cells and almost 150 wasps of the same sex can hatch from a single egg.

● **The smallest insect,** the fairyfly, is an egg parasite wasp. A fairyfly measures only about 0.2 mm.

● **A parasitic wasp can be infested** by a smaller parasitic wasp, which in turn can be infested by another wasp. This phenomenon is known as hyperparasitism.

● **Unlike other social wasps and bees,** parasitic wasps do not sting.

● **Aphids that serve as hosts** for parasitic wasps appear puffy and hard. They are known as aphid mummies, and die once the wasp larvae are ready to pupate.

● **Parasitic wasps are useful to us** because their hosts are pest insects.

◀ The Ichneumon wasp has larvae that grow and develop inside their living host, only killing the host when they are nearly fully grown and ready to pupate.

Velvet ant

- **These wasps resemble** huge hairy ants, which is why they are known as velvet ants.

- **Velvet ants are usually** red, brown or black in colour.

- **Found in dry areas,** velvet ants are densely covered with long, whitish hair. When it is too hot to venture outside, velvet ants burrow underground or climb into plants.

- **Male velvet ants** have wings and cannot sting. Females, on the other hand, do not have wings and can sting. They move about on the ground like ants and their sting can be quite painful.

- **Velvet ants have a tough outer covering,** which protects them against bee and wasp stings.

- **Female velvet ants** move swiftly and are often found searching for the burrows of solitary bees and wasps.

- **Velvet ants lay eggs** in the nests of bees and other wasps and are parasitic in nature.

- **The larva of the velvet ant** emerges before the eggs of its host hatch. It eats its host's eggs as well as its larvae.

- **Velvet ants make a squeaky noise** if they are attacked or captured.

- **The sting of the velvet ant** is powerful and people used to believe it could kill a cow. This, however, is not true.

◀ The females lay their eggs in bumblebee nests and the velvet ant larvae feed on the bee larvae.

Butterfly lifestyle

- **Butterflies do not have** a mouth or teeth to chew their food. Instead they have a strawlike structure called a proboscis, which helps them suck nectar.

- **A butterfly's wings** are covered with microscopic scales, which overlap like roof tiles.

- **Butterflies are active** during the day and fly only in the daytime. Some tropical butterflies also fly at night.

- **Adult butterflys lay eggs on plants.** The eggs hatch into caterpillars, or larvae. The caterpillar develops into a pupa or chrysalis and finally matures into a butterfly.

- **Caterpillars grow at a tremendous rate.** They shed their skin (moult) occasionally as the skin does not expand with their growth.

- **Most caterpillars moult four or five times** before they enter the pupa or chrysalis stage.

- **Butterflies do not have lungs.** Instead, they breathe through small holes in their abdomen, which are called spiracles.

- **In some species,** the caterpillars have stinging hairs containing poisons, which cause pain when touched.

- **Some male butterflies** have scent pockets on their wings, which disperse pheromones.

- **Some butterflies migrate** in order to avoid bad weather, overcrowding, or to find a new place to live.

▲ A butterfly drinking nectar from a flower using its proboscis.

Butterfly features

● **Butterflies are beautiful insects** that belong to the order Lepidoptera. About 28,000 species of butterfly have been identified so far.

● **The earliest butterfly fossils** can be traced back to the Cretaceous Period, 130 million years ago.

● **Butterflies can live anywhere in the world** except in cold regions, such as Antarctica. They cannot withstand cold weather and have to maintain a body temperature above 30°C.

● **Like other insects,** butterflies have an exoskeleton, a hard outer covering that protects the body. A butterfly's body is also divided into three sections – head, thorax and abdomen. All butterflies have a pair of compound eyes.

● **The average lifespan of butterflies** is 20 to 40 days but some species can survive up to 10 months while others last only three to four days.

▼ *Butterflies, such as this small postman butterfly, usually hold their wings upright when they rest. Moths usually spread their wings out or fold them flat.*

▼ *All butterflies have similarly shaped bodies, but the markings on their wings depend on their habitat. This comma butterfly, with its ragged wings and mottled colour, is well-camouflaged as a dead leaf, which protects it from predators.*

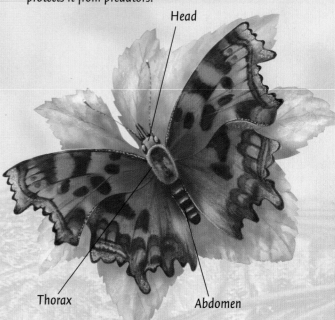

Head

Thorax

Abdomen

● **Butterflies only consume liquid food,** such as flower nectar and liquids from rotten fruits or vines. Some feed on liquid animal waste.

● **Butterflies protect themselves from predators,** such as birds, lizards, bats and spiders, by mimicry and camouflage.

● **After bees,** butterflies are the second largest pollinators of crops.

● **Some butterflies can be destructive too.** Cabbage white butterflies feed on cabbages and can destroy entire crops.

★ STAR FACT ★
Male butterflies attract the females by dancing around them. This is called a 'courtship dance'. While dancing, males secrete pheromones, a chemical scent that stimulates mating.

Tortoiseshell butterfly

- **Tortoiseshell butterflies** are brightly coloured and are found all over the world. They are one of the most common butterflies in the UK.

- **Tortoiseshell butterflies can also be found** in the hill forests of Asia and northern USA.

- **Adult tortoiseshell butterflies** feed on fruit juices or the nectar from flowers, such as daisy and aster.

- **Female tortoiseshell butterflies** are larger than the male butterflies.

- **After mating,** a female tortoiseshell butterfly lays her eggs in batches of 60 to 100 on young nettle leaves.

- **The eggs hatch after about 10 days** and the caterpillars spin a web over the nettle's growing tip. Tortoiseshell caterpillars live in groups and feed on the nettle leaves.

◄ *Tortoiseshell butterflies have a long life as adults, surviving for about 10 months.*

- **Tortoiseshell caterpillars** grow to about 2 cm in length in a month. They are black, with two yellow lines along their sides.

- **Tortoiseshell butterfly pupae** are greyish brown and have metallic spots.

- **Tortoiseshell butterflies** used to be known as the 'devil's butterfly' in Scotland.

★ **STAR FACT** ★
Tortoiseshell butterflies hibernate during the winter. Adults often hibernate in houses and sheds and can be spotted in the open between March and October, while caterpillars are seen between May to August.

Red admiral butterfly

★ **STAR FACT** ★
Red admiral butterflies prefer woods, gardens, parks, marshes and fields. During migration, these butterflies can be found in almost any habitat, from the tundra in Canada to subtropical countries near the Equator.

◄ *The red admiral butterfly's name comes from its bright, 'admirable' colours.*

- **Female red admiral butterflies** lay their eggs on nettle leaves. After seven days, the caterpillar emerges and folds leaves around itself to make a protective tent. The leaves are held together with silk threads and the caterpillar feeds inside its leaf shelter.

- **The red admiral butterfly** is easy to recognize. It is black with red bands and white markings on the wings.

- **Red Admirals are easily found** in gardens, orchards and woodlands across Europe, North America and Asia.

- **Adult red admiral butterflies** feed on flowers and rotting fruits, while caterpillars feed on nettle plants.

- **This species is known** for its migratory behaviour. Red admiral butterflies cannot survive cold winters. Once the winter sets in, they migrate to warmer places.

- **The red admiral has a very erratic,** rapid flight. Unusually for a butterfly, it sometimes flies at night.

- **The caterpillars** are black to greenish-grey in colour and have a yellow line running along each side.

- **Adult red admiral butterflies may hibernate** in winter, storing enough fat in their bodies for survival.

- **Red admiral butterflies feed on tree sap,** rotting fruit, bird droppings. and the nectar of plants, such as common milkweed, red clover, aster and alfalfa.

Monarch butterfly

- **Monarch butterflies** are found all over the world, except in the cold regions. They are black and orange in colour and have a wingspan ranging up to 10 cm.

- **Monarch butterflies use their body colour** to frighten off their enemies. The orange colour is considered a warning sign. They can also blend easily with the surroundings.

- **Monarch caterpillars feed on milkweed plants,** retaining the sap in their bodies even when they mature into butterflies. Birds attempting to eat monarchs dislike the taste and spit them out.

- **Monarchs are beneficial for crops** as they eat milkweed plants, which are weeds.

- **Monarch caterpillars are brightly coloured,** with white spots around the margin of their wings. They are voracious eaters.

- **Male monarch butterflies** have dark spots called scent scales on their hind wings. Females do not have scent scales.

- **A monarch butterfly takes approximately one month** to mature from an egg into an adult butterfly. Adult monarch butterflies feed on flower nectar and water.

- **They are long distance migratory insects** and can migrate over 3200 km. Monarch butterflies guide themselves during migration using the position of the Sun and the magnetic field of the Earth.

- **Habitat destruction and changes caused by logging** are constant threats to monarch butterflies. Spraying of pesticides for weed control kills milkweed plants. This endangers the habitat and food source for these butterflies.

▲ Canadians call this butterfly 'King Billy' because its orange and black colours are the same as those of King William of Orange, who was king of Great Britain from 1689–1702.

★ STAR FACT ★
Monarch butterflies from northern USA and Canada migrate to the Sierra Madre Mountains, west of Mexico City, Mexico in the winter. The location was first discovered in 1975.

▲ The white spots on the head and thorax of monarch butterflies act as an extra warning signal, which emphasizes to birds and reptiles that this butterfly tastes horrible.

Bhutan glory butterfly

- **Bhutan glory butterflies** are found in Bhutan and north-eastern parts of Asia.

- **These butterflies prefer to live** in grass fields and undisturbed forests.

- **The wings of Bhutan glory butterflies** are black and measure about 9 to 11 cm.

- **Bhutan glory butterflies breed twice a year** from May to June and from August to October.

- **Very little is known** about the life history of Bhutan glory butterflies.

- **Experts believe** that these insects probably feed on the poisonous Indian birthwort plant.

- **Bhutan glory butterflies protect themselves** from predators by absorbing poison from the plants they feed on.

- **These butterflies fly at altitudes** of 1700–3000 m in the mountains.

- **Bhutan glory butterflies were collected** in large numbers in the past. Now, their numbers have been greatly reduced and they are very rare to spot.

- **Bhutan glory butterflies are now listed** as an endangered and protected species.

◄ At rest, the Bhutan glory butterfly hides its colourful back wings with its front wings so it is well camouflaged. If disturbed, this butterfly quickly opens and shuts it wings, exposing its bright orange markings. These sudden flashes of colour may confuse a predator and allow the butterfly time to escape.

Painted lady butterfly

★ STAR FACT ★
Painted lady butterflies do not survive in winter. They die in the cold weather.

- **The painted lady butterfly** is also known as the thistle butterfly, as its caterpillar feeds mostly on thistle plants, and as cosmopolite because it is found worldwide.

- **The painted lady is one of the best-known** butterflies in the world.

- **Painted lady butterflies are mostly found** in temperate regions across Asia, Europe and North America.

▶ The painted lady butterfly has white marks on the black tips of its front wings.

- **These butterflies are primarily** black, brown and orange in colour. They have a wingspan of 4 to 5 cm.

- **Female painted lady butterflies lay eggs** on plants, such as thistles. After three to five days, they hatch into caterpillars. The caterpillars transform into pupae and finally emerge as colourful adult butterflies.

- **The caterpillar, or larva,** lives in a silky nest woven around the plant on which it feeds.

- **Adult painted lady butterflies feed on nectar** from flowers, such as aster, cosmos, ironweed and joe-pye weed.

- **An adult painted lady butterfly lives** for only two weeks.

- **Painted lady butterflies are strong fliers** and long-distance migrants. They can travel thousands of kilometres, sometimes with thousands of individuals flying together.

Birdwing butterfly

- **Female Queen Alexandra's birdwing butterflies** are the world's largest butterflies. They can grow up to 8 cm in length.

- **Birdwing butterflies belong to** the swallowtail group of butterflies. The butterflies have tails on their hind wings, like the wings of a swallow.

- **Male birdwing butterflies** are brightly coloured with yellow, pale blue and green markings.

- **Female birdwing butterflies** have cream and chocolate brown markings on their wings.

- **Predators avoid birdwing butterflies** because they are poisonous and distasteful. Birdwing caterpillars feed on the pipevine plants and absorb poisons from these plants.

- **A birdwing butterfly lives** for about seven months.

> ★ STAR FACT ★
> Queen Alexandra's birdwing butterflies were named in honour of the wife of King Edward VII of England.

- **The birdwing butterfly is listed** as an endangered species. People are not allowed to hunt this insect.

- **The golden birdwing** and southern birdwing are some of the cousins of the Queen Alexandra's birdwing butterfly.

- **Birdwing butterflies are found** in tropical areas. The best time to spot these butterflies is in the early morning when they collect nectar from flowers.

◀ The beautiful Rajah Brooke's birdwing soars high in the rainforest canopy from Malaysia through to Sumatra and Borneo.

Apollo butterfly

- **Apollo butterflies** are mostly found in hilly regions of Spain, central Europe, southern Scandinavia and Asia. Some live above an altitude of 4000 m and rarely descend to lower levels.

- **Apollo butterflies are cream in colour** with red and yellow eyespots on their wings. They are frail-looking butterflies but survive harsh weather conditions.

- **Habitat destruction** has made Apollo butterflies extremely rare. They are now an endangered species, protected by law in many countries.

- **The breeding season** of Apollo butterflies lasts from July to August. The female lays hundreds of eggs.

- **An adult Apollo butterfly** has a lifespan of a week.

- **Apollo caterpillars feed on** stonecrop plants.

◀ This mountain butterfly has a wingspan of 50 to 100 mm and a furry body to protect it from the cold.

- **Female butterflies lay round,** white eggs. The eggs usually hatch in the months of August and September.

- **These caterpillars moult five times** in their lifetime.

- **Attempts are being made** to save Apollo butterfly populations by means of habitat management measures, reduction of insecticide use and observation of their behaviour during the time they are on the wing.

> ★ STAR FACT ★
> Adult butterflies use their proboscis, a kind of sucking tube, to feed on nectar from flowers, such as the thistle.

Peacock butterfly

◀ *Peacock butterflies use the false eyes on their wings to scare predators away.*

★ STAR FACT ★
Peacock butterflies hibernate to avoid harsh winters. They take refuge in places such as hollow trees, rock crevices or stone walls. If disturbed, they create a hissing sound by rubbing their wings together.

● **Peacock butterflies** are named after their large, multi-coloured spots, which look like the 'eyes' on a real peacock's feathers. Adult peacock butterflies are light to dark brown in colour and have purplish-black lines.

● **These butterflies live** in temperate areas of Europe and Asia. They are commonly found in England and Wales.

● **Adult peacock butterflies** love to be around orchards, gardens and other places that have lots of flowers. They feed on the flower nectar of thistles, lavender and buddleia and also suck juices from overripe fruits.

● **Peacock caterpillars** feed on nettle plants.

● **Peacock butterflies live in groups.** They have a single brood in a year. Adults hibernate through the winter and emerge in the spring. They die after laying eggs.

● **Female peacock butterflies lay** up to 500 eggs. The caterpillars emerge after one to two weeks.

● **Fully grown caterpillars** are about 4 cm long. They have black-and-white spots and long black dorsal spines.

● **The pupae are** greyish-brown, with metallic gold spots.

● **The lifespan of a peacock butterfly** is relatively long and can even last up to one year.

Viceroy butterfly

● **Viceroy butterflies** are mostly found in the USA, southern Canada and northern Mexico.

● **They have black and orange patterns** with white spots on their wings.

● **These butterflies are found** in meadows, marshes and swamps and other wet areas with trees, such as willow, aspen and poplar.

● **There are usually two or three generations** of viceroy butterflies born in each breeding season.

● **Viceroy butterflies mate** in the afternoon. The female butterfly lays her eggs on poplar and willow leaves.

● **These eggs hatch** and the viceroy caterpillars feed on the leaves of trees such as willow and poplar.

● **The caterpillars are white** and olive brown.

● **Adult viceroy butterflies feed on** the liquids from decaying fungi, dung and other animal waste.

◀ *The viceroy has a faster wingbeat than the monarch butterfly and also glides with its wings held horizontally, not held at an angle like the monarch.*

● **Predators often mistake viceroy butterflies** for monarch butterflies, and avoid eating them. Viceroy butterflies are not poisonous.

★ STAR FACT ★
Butterflies practice two kinds of mimicry – Batesian and Mullerian. In Batesian mimicry, a harmless species of butterfly mimics a toxic species. In Mullerian mimicry, two equally toxic species mimic each other for mutual benefit. Viceroy and monarch butterflies exhibit Batesian mimicry.

Moths

- **Moths make up about 90 percent** of the insects that belong to order Lepidoptera, which also includes butterflies. Insects that belong to this order have scaly wings.

- **Moths feed on nectar** as well as other plant juices. Some moths do not feed as adults because they do not have mouthparts.

- **In some species of moth,** the females do not have wings.

- **Most moths** are active only at night.

- **Like butterflies,** some moths, such as hawk-moths, migrate long distances.

- **Some moths have large spots** on their wings. From a distance, these spots resemble the eyes of a fearsome animal and scare away potential predators.

◀ The Polyphemus moth has striking eyespots on its back wings and is named after the one-eyed giant of Greek myths.

- **Moths are masters** of mimicry and camouflage.

- **Some moths can be mistaken for** bird droppings when they lie still on the ground. This helps them escape to the eyes of predatory birds.

- **Species of moths known as clothes moth** are quite unusual. The larvae of these moths are destructive in nature and feed on different types of natural fabrics, such as wool, cotton, linen and even on fur, feathers and hair.

★ STAR FACT ★
Tiger moths produce supersonic sound just like bats. These moths are known for their awful taste and bats avoid eating them.

Death's head hawk-moth

- **Death's head hawk-moths** belong to a group called sphinx moths, and are found in Africa, Asia and Europe.

- **This moth is named after** a peculiar mark, which is visible on its thorax. The mark looks like a skull.

- **Death's head hawk-moths steal honey** from bees' nests, which is why they are also known as 'bee robbers'.

- **At any point in its growth stage,** a death's head hawk-moth is capable of producing a loud squeaking sound to scare its predators away.

- **These moths force air** out of their strong, thick proboscis to make this squeaky sound.

- **Females lay single eggs** on different plants. They prefer to lay their eggs on potato and brinjal plants.

- **The caterpillars have a horn on their tail end** and are also known as hornworms.

- **To pupate,** the caterpillars make a mud cell deep in the soil and smoothe it by pushing their head against the wall of the cell.

▲ The caterpillars of Death's head hawk-moths reach 12.5 cm when fully grown and make a clicking sound if disturbed.

- **Death's head hawk-moths find it difficult** to survive harsh winters and migrate to warmer places.

★ STAR FACT ★
The strange mark on the thorax of the death's head hawk-moth has given rise to many superstitions. In ancient times the presence of this moth was considered a sign of death.

Atlas moth

- **Atlas moths** belong to the group of emperor moths and are known for their large size. They are named because the patterns on their wings look like maps.

- **Atlas moths are the largest moths,** with a wingspan of 24 to 30 cm. When they fly, they are often mistaken for birds.

- **Atlas moths are found** in forests in south-east Asia.

- **The tips of their wings** are hooked and have patterns on them, which helps to scare predators away.

- **Females are much larger and heavier** than the males, and their antennae are less hairy.

- **Females lay eggs under leaves.** These eggs hatch into greenish caterpillars, which feed on leaves.

- **Adults do not have mouthparts** so they cannot eat. They live for just two weeks and die soon after mating.

◀ Giant Atlas moths have transparent triangles in the middle of each wing where the coloured scales are missing. These shiny patches may confuse predators by reflecting the light.

- **Males have large feathery antennae.** These antennae are capable of sensing pheromones released by female atlas moths from a distance of several kilometres.

- **The caterpillars have fleshy projections** all over their bodies, and can grow up to 12 cm in length.

> ★ STAR FACT ★
> Atlas moth cocoons hang from trees like fruits. These cocoons are used to produce a type of silk in Asia, known as Fagara silk.

Swallowtail moth

- **Swallowtail moths** belong to the family geometridae of the order Lepidoptera.

- **Swallowtail moths** are strikingly unusual and can be mistaken for butterflies. They have slender bodies, thin legs and a short proboscis.

- **These moths** sometimes fly during the day.

- **Swallowtail moths** are very large in size and are found mainly in tropical countries.

- **In June and July,** swallowtail moths are widespread and common in Europe and parts of Asia.

- **Not much is known** about the life history of swallowtail moths.

- **Some of the nocturnal species** have eyespots at the tip of their short pointed hind wings.

◀ This large moth has broad wings, like a butterfly, but flies rapidly.

- **These eyespots give an impression** of a false head at the rear side of the moth, which protects it from predators. Therefore, during the day, these moths always rest on the upper side of leaves.

- **The size and marks** on the bodies differ in male and female swallowtail moths.

> ★ STAR FACT ★
> Swallowtail moths derive their names from their resemblance to swallowtail butterflies. Their hindwings have a tail similar to that of swallowtail butterflies.

Hummingbird hawk-moth

● **Hummingbird hawk-moths** belong to the hawk-moth group and are found all over the world.

● **Unlike other hawk-moths,** these moths fly during the day and can be easily spotted hovering over flowers in gardens and parks.

● **Brownish in colour,** hummingbird hawk-moths have black-and-white spots all over their body and their hind wings are orange.

● **These moths have a brown,** white-spotted abdomen with tufts of hair at the tip.

● **Like other butterflies and moths,** hummingbird hawk-moths have long, tubelike mouthparts that are coiled and tucked under their head.

● **These moths use their long tongue** to collect nectar from flowers.

● **The caterpillar is slender and colourful.** It has a horned tail, which gives it a fearsome look.

● **The moth pupates** in leaf litter (dead leaves, bits of bark, and other dead plant matter lying on the ground), and weaves a very thick cocoon.

● **People often mistake this moth** for a hummingbird because it hovers over flowers and sucks nectar from them, like a hummingbird.

● **Hummingbird hawk-moths** hibernate in winter to survive the cold weather.

▼ *The broad body of this robust little hawk-moth shows that it is a powerful flier. It holds its body still while hovering in front of flowers, beating its wings so fast that they are almost invisible. The rapidly beating wings produce a high-pitched hum, like the wings of a hummingbird.*

Lobster moth

● **Lobster moths** belong to the group of moths known as prominent moths.

● **These moths are commonly found** in deciduous forests in Europe and Asia.

● **The wingspan of lobster moths** is about 5.5 to 7 cm.

● **Males are often attracted** to light, but females are not.

▶ *A lobster moth caterpillar confuses predators by suddenly changing shape. It raises its head and tail over its body (making it look like a tiny lobster) and waves a pair of filaments at the end of its abdomen. Lobster moth caterpillars can also squirt formic acid over their predators.*

● **This moth appears in two colour forms** – one with light front wings and one with dark front wings.

● **Lobster moths move in a way** that resembles the movements of ants.

● **The unusual shape of lobster moth caterpillars** often confuses their predators and scares them away.

● **As an act of defence,** the caterpillar curls back its large head and raises its legs in the air to startle small birds.

● **The caterpillar constructs a silken cocoon** and pupates in it.

★ STAR FACT ★
Lobster moths are so-called as their larvae have six wiry, elongated legs and a swollen tale like a lobster.

Peppered moth

● **Peppered moths** belong to a group of moths known as geometrid moths.

● **These moths are delicate insects** and have long legs and a slender body.

● **Peppered moth caterpillars** do not have any legs in the middle of their body. They hold onto branches with their first two pairs of specialized limbs called prolegs and a clasper at their tail end.

● **The antennae of male peppered moths** are feathery, and are longer thn those of the females.

● **Males are smaller and more slender** in comparison with the larger and heavier female peppered moths.

● **There are two varieties of peppererd moths;** a paler coloured variety, speckled with salt and pepper (black-and-white) marks while the other is coal-black in colour.

● **Peppered moths are nocturnal** and usually rest on barks of lichen-covered trees during the day.

◀ *The pale form of the peppered moth is more easily seen against dark backgrounds. The wingspan is 50 to 60 mm.*

● **Peppered moth caterpillars camouflage themselves** by resembling a twig.

● **During the Industrial Revolution,** the barks of many trees became blackish-grey in colour due to air pollution. Dark-coloured peppered moths blended with this environment and matched the colour of the tree bark. Paler peppered moths stood out as targets for birds and other predators so more dark-coloured moths survived.

★ STAR FACT ★
Peppered moth caterpillars are known as inchworms because they move their bodies in a looping fashion as though they are measuring the earth.

Moon moth

- **Moon moths** belong to the group known as Emperor moths. They live all over the world, but are mostly seen in tropical countries.

- **Moon moths have a white body** and maroon legs.

- **The wings of the moon moth** are bright green in colour. The colour of female moon moths is brighter than that of the males.

- **Moon moths have a wingspan** of about 10 to 13 cm and their tail is almost 8 cm long.

- **The hind wings of males** are longer than the females'. In overall size, male moon moths are smaller than females.

- **An adult female** lays about 250 eggs at a time, on walnut leaves. The eggs resemble seeds with grey specks on them.

- **Adult moon moths** have no mouthparts and do not eat anything. They do not live for more than a week.

◀ The eyespots on the wings of moon moths probably help to divert the attention of predators away from the moth's delicate body.

- **Moon moths make their cocoons in leaves.** The silk of the cocoon does not shine and is brown in colour.

- **Moon moth caterpillars** are bright green in colour and are beautifully segmented, with some white hairs.

> ★ STAR FACT ★
> Moon moths are also called 'lunar moths' because of marks on their wings that look like a new moon.

Vinegar fly

- **Vinegar flies** are tiny insects and measure about 2 mm in length.

- **Vinegar flies are also called pomace flies** because they are attracted by the sour smell of pomace, which is the liquid squeezed from fruit or seeds.

- **These insects have large red eyes** and their bodies are brownish yellow in colour.

- **Vinegar flies are not strong fliers** and can cover only short distances but these lightweight insects are easily carried along by the wind.

- **Vinegar flies are used extensively** for genetic research because their cells are strikingly similar to those of humans. Around 60 percent of their genes match with those of humans.

◀ Adult vinegar flies live for just two weeks, feeding on nectar and other sugary solutions.

- **A female vinegar fly** can lay around 200 eggs if conditions are suitable.

- **The eggs laid by female vinegar flies** are not easily visible to the human eye. These eggs are normally found near decaying and fermented fruits and vegetables.

- **The larvae feed on fermented food materials.** They pupate and develop into adult flies in four to five days.

- **Several generations can be produced** in a couple of weeks, which is why these insects are suitable for scientific studies.

- **Vinegar flies are considered pests** because they can transmit germs and diseases from decaying food materials.

Horse fly

- **Horse flies** are strong-bodied flies with colourful patterns on their bodies.

- **Horse flies suck and feed** on the blood of humans and animals. These insects get their names, such as deer flies or moose flies, depending on the animal they feed on.

- **There are about** 25,000 species of horse fly.

- **Horse flies have compound eyes,** which are very prominent and occupy the entire surface of head in the males.

- **Colourful patterns** on the compound eyes are caused by the refraction of light. There are no pigments present in the eyes.

- **The mouthparts of these insects** consist of a short powerful, piercing organ capable of penetrating tough skin. If undisturbed, horse flies can suck blood from their host for as long as half an hour.

- **After mating,** females lay their eggs on plant and rock edges near water. The eggs are creamy white in colour.

- **Female horse flies bite other animals** to suck blood before they reproduce. Male horse flies do not bite. They feed mainly on flower nectar and plant sap.

- **Horse fly larvae** feed on soft-bodied insects and other small animals. They can become cannibalistic if there is a lack of food.

- **While biting and sucking blood** from animals, horse flies can transmit diseases such as anthrax.

◄ Horse flies are among the fastest flying insects, reaching maximum speeds of 39 km/h. Unlike most other flies, their flight can be silent, allowing females to sneak up on their prey.

Crane fly

► The long, thin legs of a crane fly are often twice as long as its body. Crane flies can also be recognized by the V-shaped groove on the top of their thorax.

- **Crane flies** belong to order Diptera and are closely related to mosquitoes.

- **These long-legged insects** are also known as 'daddy long legs'. Their legs are weakly attached to their body and often break off.

- **Some of the larger species of crane fly** have legs that are as long as 2.5 cm.

- **Crane flies have extremely narrow wings.** They have a thin body and long legs and resemble large mosquitoes. These insects cannot bite.

- **Crane flies are nocturnal insects** and remain inactive in the day.

- **Females lay their eggs** in moist soil. The eggs hatch into larvae, which are greyish to pale brown in colour.

- **The larvae of crane flies** feed on dead and decaying matter. Some species also feed on other small insects and others eat plant roots.

- **Crane fly larvae are also known as** leatherjackets because of their tough, brown skin. They are often used as fishing bait.

- **Farmers dislike the larvae** of these insects because they damage the roots and turf of grain fields and grass crops.

- **A rare species of crane fly** does not have wings. These insects are found in Hawaii.

House-fly

- **House-flies** belong to the order Diptera and are one of the most common insects.

- **House-flies have small projections** below their front wings known as halteres. Halteres are modified hind wings, which are used for landing and balancing.

- **House-flies feed on liquid food** and do not bite animals and other insects. The mouthparts of a house-fly are like a sponge, which absorbs liquid food.

- **House-flies will vomit** a portion of their last feed onto new food particles. This makes new food easier to digest.

- **Most of the time,** house-flies do not eat all the food and leave some particles behind. These remaining food particles can spread a variety of diseases.

- **House-flies are considered** to be the most dangerous vector. A vector is an organism which carries disease-causing micro-organisms from host to host.

- **House-flies have compound eyes,** and each eye has 4000 individual lenses. They cannot see the colour red.

> ★ STAR FACT ★
> House-flies are known to spread forty serious diseases. A single fly harbours as many as 500,000,000 on its body surface and legs.

◀ Sticky pads and sharp claws enable house-flies to walk upside down with ease. Fine hairs on the tip of a house fly's legs also enable it to 'taste' liquids.

- **Female house-flies** can lay more than 600 to 1000 eggs in a lifetime, but most offspring do not survive to reproduce.

- **Common house-flies** are normally found wherever there is human activity. They thrive on the waste materials left behind by humans and other animals.

Mosquito

- **Mosquitoes are the only flies** of the order Diptera that have scaly wings.

- **Most female mosquitoes** have to feed on the blood of other animals to reproduce. They need the protein extracted from blood for the development of their eggs.

◀ A female mosquito uses her needle-like mouthparts to pierce a victim's skin and suck up a blood meal. She injects a salivary fluid to keep the blood flowing and stop it from the clotting.

- **The eggs float on water** and hatch to produce aquatic larvae known as wrigglers.

- **The larvae cannot breathe underwater** and 'hang' from the water's surface to take in air.

- **Mosquito larvae pupate** in the water itself. The pupa is not completely immobile. It can change position according to the light and wind conditions in its environment.

- **Adult male mosquitoes** feed on nectar and other plant fluids. Only female mosquitoes feed on blood.

- **Male mosquitoes cannot bite.** Their mouthparts are modified for sucking only.

- **Mosquitoes have infrared vision.** They can sense the warmth of other insects and animals.

- **Dragonflies feed on mosquitoes** and are also known as mosquito hawks. Dragonfly nymphs also feed on mosquito larvae.

- **Mosquitoes are known to spread many infectious diseases,** such as yellow fever and dengue fever. The female Anopheles mosquito spreads malaria.

Firefly

● **Fireflies are actually a type of beetle.** They are also known as lightning bugs.

● **Fireflies grow** up to 2.5 cm in length and live for three to four months. Female fireflies live longer than males.

● **Fireflies have a special organ** under their belly, which emits flashes of green or yellow light.

● **The light is known as 'cold light'.** This process of producing light is also known as bioluminescence. No other insects can produce light from their own bodies.

● **Fireflies emit only light energy.** A light bulb emits only 10 percent of the energy as light. The remaining 90 percent is emitted as heat energy.

● **Female fireflies and their larvae** are carnivorous and feed on snails, slugs and worms. Most male fireflies don't eat but some feed on pollen and nectar.

★ STAR FACT ★
Some female fireflies fool males of other species by flickering their light. When the males come closer to mate, the females eat them.

● **Male and female fireflies** emit light to attract mates.

● **Fireflies are nocturnal in nature.** They live on plants and trees during the day and are active at night.

● **Some female fireflies** are wingless and are also known as glow-worms.

◀ *A female firefly signals to a mate with her glowing tail.*

Goliath beetle

● **The Goliath beetle** is one of the largest and heaviest insects in the world. Males are as heavy as an apple.

● **Goliath beetles grow up to** 12 cm and weigh about 115 g.

● **Found in many colours,** most Goliath beetles have black and white spots on their wings.

● **Goliath beetles used to be found** only in Africa. Today, however, these insects can be found in almost all parts of the world.

● **Males have a horn-shaped structure** on their heads. They often fight each other with their horns.

● **Goliath beetles are good fliers.** They produce a low, helicopter-like whir while flying.

● **By feeding on dead plant and animal tissues,** Goliath beetles help to keep the environment clean.

● **A fossil of the oldest goliath beetle** dates is almost 300 million years old.

● **Scientists believe that goliath beetles,** like some other insects, were much larger in prehistoric times. This may because there was more oxygen in the air long ago.

▶ *The male Goliath beetle would only just fit on your hand! Adult beetles cannot grow, which means that Goliath beetles also have giant larvae.*

★ STAR FACT ★
The Goliath beetle is named after the Biblical giant, Goliath.

Bombardier beetle

- **Bombardier beetles** are ground beetles. They have a black body and yellow-spotted wings.

- **The wing covers of bombardier beetles** are fused together. They cannot fly but they are very fast runners.

- **Bombardier beetles have an interesting defence strategy.** Two separate chambers within the beetle's body contain chemicals – hydrogen peroxide and hydroquinone.

- **These chemicals fuse together** to form a noxious toxin, which causes irritation.

- **The temperature of this toxic liquid** is 100 °C. It is squirted out from the beetle's body straight away, otherwise it would explode.

▶ The bombardier beetle can twist the end of its abdomen to squirt out a poisonous spray. This gives the insect time to escape.

- **Bombardier beetles use a cannon-like body part** in their abdomen to spray the liquid at their predators.

- **The liquid evaporates** after it is sprayed, forming a gas that temporarily blinds the enemy, while the bombardier beetle runs away.

- **Bombardier beetles spend most of their time** in rotting wood and lay eggs on plant remains and other decomposing matter.

- **These beetles are scavengers** and come out at night. Their larvae are carnivorous and feed on other insects.

★ STAR FACT ★
The bombardier beetle inspired Germans to use jet propulsion to spray noxious toxins on their enemies during World War II.

Tiger beetle

- **Tiger beetles are usually shiny metallic colours,** such as green, black and purple. They often have stripes just like tigers.

- **The smallest tiger beetles** live in Borneo and measure up to 6 mm. The largest tiger beetles live in Africa and are as large as 44 mm.

- **Tiger beetles are found in** sandy areas and are usually active during the day. There are some species that come out at night.

- **Tiger beetles are good fliers** and will fly in a zigzag pattern if a predator approaches. They are also very fast runners.

◀ Tiger beetles have huge eyes with which to see their prey and massive biting jaws to catch and cut up their food.

- **These insects are predatory in nature.** Once they locate their prey, they pounce on it and use their jaws to tear it into pieces.

- **Tiger beetles taste awful** and their predators avoid eating them.

- **Female tiger beetles lay their eggs** in burrows in the ground. The burrow can be almost 0.5 m deep.

- **The larvae of tiger beetles** have a pair of powerful and large jaws, which are used to capture small insects.

- **Some species of tiger beetles** are endangered or nearing extinction. This is because of the lack of undisturbed sandy areas in which they can breed.

★ STAR FACT ★
In Borneo, a type of locust mimics tiger beetles to save itself from its predators.

Diving beetle

● **Diving beetles** have an oval body, which is brown or black in colour. Their wings are shiny and look metallic green when light reflects off their body. Diving beetles are commonly found in ponds and other still water.

● **A diving beetle has strong hairy legs,** which it uses like the oars of a rowing boat to push its body forwards while swimming.

● **These insects cannot breathe underwater** and have to come to the water's surface to breathe air. They store this air under their wing covers.

● **Diving beetles often fly at night** in search of new ponds.

● **The beetles locate new ponds** with the help of the light that reflects from water surfaces. They often get confused with light that is reflected from a glass surface and mistake it for water.

● **The female diving beetle** is much bigger in size than the male beetle.

● **Females make small slits** in a plant stem and lay their eggs inside.

● **The larvae float on the surface of the pond** and move to the shore to pupate.

● **The larvae are known as 'water tigers'** because they can attack and bite other insects. They can even eat tadpoles and small fish.

● **Diving beetles feed on** other water insects, small fishes and tadpoles.

▼ *The great diving beetle has a flattened, streamlined body, which helps it to swim rapidly. It moves its back legs together, rather than alternately like most other water beetles. When the beetle stops swimming, it floats to the surface of the water.*

Stag beetle

- **Stag beetles** are usually brown or black in colour but there are some species that are bright green and red.

- **These beetles live in damp wooded areas,** especially near oak woodlands.

- **Stag beetles have mandibles** (jaws), which look similar to the antlers of a stag.

- **Males have long and ferocious looking jaws.** The jaws of females are not as long as those of the males.

- **Males use their antlers** to attract females. They rarely use their jaws to fight.

- **At dusk, male stag beetles** fly in search of females to mate. They often get misguided by bright lights.

> ★ STAR FACT ★
> Stag beetles are also known as 'pinching bugs' because they can nip with their jaws and draw blood from people.

- **The larvae of these insects** feed on rotten wood and plant remains.

- **The larvae take a long time** to develop into mature adults because their food is not nutritious.

- **Adult stag beetles** feed on the sap of trees.

◄ Lesser stag beetles have smaller jaws than the larger elephant or giant stag beetles. Stag beetles are one of the 20,000 species in the scarab beetle superfamily.

Rhinoceros beetle

- **Rhinoceros beetles** are believed to be proportionally the strongest creatures on Earth. They can carry about 850 times their own weight.

- **These beetles** can grow up to 13 cm in length.

- **The preferred habitat of rhinoceros beetles** is tropical rainforests where the vegetation is thick and there is plenty of moisture in the atmosphere.

- **Rhinoceros beetles are named after** the horns on their head, which resemble spikes.

- **Only males have horns.** The larger the horn, the better are their chances of winning a mate's attention.

- **The horns are very strong** and can pierce through the exoskeletons of insects.

- **Rhinoceros beetles do not use their horns** for defending themselves from predators. They use them to fight other males for food and to attract female beetles for mating.

◄ This rhinoceros beetle has two horns, but some have three, or even five, horns. The very tough exoskeleton protects the beetle's body like a suit of armour.

- **Rhinoceros beetles are nocturnal** in nature and almost all their hunting and feeding activities take place at night.

- **These beetles help to keep the jungle clean** and feed on plant sap and rotten fruits that have fallen on the ground.

- **Rhinoceros beetles are known to be fierce fighters.** Natives in some parts of Thailand hold beetle fighting competitions to watch these beetles fight.

Ladybird beetle

- **Ladybird beetles,** or ladybugs, were named after the Virgin Mary, because in early religious paintings she was often shown wearing a red clock. They were known as 'beetle of Our Lady' during the Medieval period.

- **Ladybirds are almost circular in shape.** They are bright pink, orange or red with black and red or orange spots. The number of spots may vary from species to species. Ladybirds are found in temperate and tropical regions all over the world.

- **These beetles are one of the most beneficial insects** because they feed on insect pests that damage crops.

- **Ladybirds are sometimes bred** on a large scale and are then introduced into farms or greenhouses to get rid of pests. However, some species of ladybirds are herbivorous and are considered pests themselves.

- **These insects are easily mistaken** for leaf beetles because of their similar colouring and spots.

- **When disturbed,** ladybirds secrete a foul smelling fluid, which causes a stain. This is called reflex-bleeding.

- **Both adults and larvae** eat aphids, scale insects and other soft-bodied insects.

- **Ladybird larvae do not have wings.** They are metallic blue in colour with bright yellow spots all over their body. Their bright colour warns birds not to eat them.

- **The halloween ladybird** is a pumpkin-orange coloured beetle found in the USA during late October. It is named after Halloween because it is often seen during this festival.

- **Adult ladybirds hibernate** in huge clusters in densely vegetated areas, usually at high altitudes.

▼ The bright colours of adult ladybirds warn predators that they taste horrible and are best left alone. Hidden under the brightly coloured wing cases are two delicate wings.

True bugs

- **True bugs belong** to the suborder Heteroptera of the order Hemiptera. There are at least 55,000 different kinds of bugs.

- **These bugs generally** have two pairs of wings. The first pair is partially hard and protects the delicate membrane-like second pair of wings.

- **Some bugs do not have wings** while the nymphs of all bugs are wingless.

- **True bugs have compound eyes** and mouthparts that are adapted for sucking and piercing.

- **Bugs undergo incomplete metamorphosis.** There is no pupal stage and the bugs grow into adults by moulting repeatedly. The nymphs resemble the adult bugs.

- **Bugs survive on land,** in air, on the surface of water and even under water.

- **Bugs feed on plant and animal juices.** There are some bugs, such as bed bugs, which are parasites. They live by sucking blood from other animals.

▲ *A true bug is an insect with piercing and sucking mouthparts, which are tucked beneath the head when not in use.*

- **Some bugs give out a bad odour.** This is a defence strategy.

- **Carnivorous bugs** are predatory and help to control pests while herbivorous bugs are a threat to crops. Bugs can also be cannibalistic.

- **Some people** cultivate certain species of bugs to obtain dyes from them, while others relish bugs as food.

Assassin bug

> ★ STAR FACT ★
> The saliva of assassin bugs can cause temporary blindness in humans.

- **Assassin bugs** are black, brown or bright red and black.

- **The wings of assassin bugs** lie flat on their abdomen. They have long legs, which are adapted for running.

- **Assassin bugs are predatory.** They grab their prey and 'assassinate' it by injecting venom. This venom is so powerful that caterpillars, which are several times larger than assassin bugs, can be killed in a few seconds.

- **The venom paralyzes the prey** and partially dissolves and disintegrates it. The bug then sucks the liquid food.

▶ *An assassin bug may take several days to eat a large victim. Its front legs have powerful muscles for holding prey.*

- **Assassin bugs have a powerful curved beak,** which is used for sucking the blood of other insects, larger animals and even humans.

- **Male and female assassin bugs** are similar in appearance but sometimes the females don't have wings.

- **Assassin bugs give out a pungent smell** and have a poisonous bite, to protect them from predators.

- **An assassin bug's bite** can be painful and can transmit germs and diseases. These bugs are known to spread a disease called Chagas' disease.

- **A species of assassin bug,** known as the masked assassin bug, camouflages itself by sticking dirt to its body.

Squash bug

● **Squash bugs** are named because they are a threat to squash and other related plants. They can usually be found in colours ranging from brown to black.

● **Some squash bugs** have leaflike extensions on their hind legs. This makes them look like dead leaves, which helps with camouflage. These bugs are called leaf-footed bugs.

● **With their powerful beaks,** squash bugs can easily pierce and suck fluids from plants and insects.

● **Squash bugs have scent glands** that emit a pungent smell. However, the odour is not as strong as that of stink bugs.

◀ The squash bug of North America feeds on the juices of cucumber, squash, melon, pumpkin and other gourds. It does not have leaflike back legs.

● **A few squash bugs** feed on both plants and insects, and some are strictly vegetarian.

● **While feeding,** the squash bug injects a toxic substance into the plant. As a result, the plant wilts and dies.

● **Squash bugs lay their eggs** in clusters on plants. The eggs are oval, flattish or elongated in shape.

● **The nymphs that hatch from these eggs** resemble black ants and moult four to five times before maturing into adults.

● **Farmers consider squash bugs** to be dangerous pests and adopt various measures to get rid of them.

> ★ STAR FACT ★
> A rice field affected by squash bugs can be smelt from a considerable distance away.

Cicada

▶ Cicada eggs hatch into wingless nymphs. Most cicadas spend between one and three years as nymphs.

● **Cicadas** belong to the order Homoptera and are related to true bugs.

● **Most species of cicada** are found in deserts, grasslands and forests.

● **Cicadas have large and colourful wings.** They hold their wings in a slanting position over their abdomen, like a tent.

● **Cicadas emit a sound** similar to that of a knife grinder, a railway whistle and even to fat spitting in an overheated pan.

● **Male cicadas sing loudly to attract females,** with the help of special drumlike membranes called timbals. Female cicadas do not produce any sound because their timbals are not developed.

> ★ STAR FACT ★
> In Borneo, Malaysia and many other areas of the South Pacific, people eat cicadas.

● **Large swarms of cicadas** attract birds, which feast on these insects.

● **Female cicadas lay their eggs** on plants and tree twigs. When the eggs hatch, the nymphs fall to the ground. The nymphs live underground for many years, feeding on the roots of plants. Later, they emerge from the ground, climb up trees and then moult.

● **Adult cicadas do not live as long as the nymphs.** They only survive a few weeks.

● **A species of cicada known as the periodical cicada** is found in America. It emerges from under the ground every 13 or 17 years. These insects are one of the longest-lived in the world.

Spittlebug

★ STAR FACT ★
In Madagascar, spittlebugs discharge a clear liquid instead of foam, which falls to the ground like rain.

● **Spittlebugs** are different shades of yellow and brown. They have a triangular head, red eyes and spotted wings.

● **Spittlebugs have a froglike appearance** and are also known as froghoppers. They are good jumpers but rarely fly, although they do have wings.

● **Adult spittlebugs** have rather large heads in comparison with their small bodies.

● **They are named after** the frothy mass secreted by the nymphs, sometimes known as cuckoo-spit.

● **Cuckoo-spit** protects the spittlebug nymphs from predators.

● **Spittlebug nymphs** are hard to spot as they are often hidden in a frothy mass on leaves.

● **The froth also helps the nymphs** to control their temperature and even prevents them from losing moisture and drying out.

● **Some spittlebug nymphs** form delicate tubes about 10 to 12 mm in length. They attach these tubes along the sides of twigs and live there after filling them with spittle.

● **Spittlebugs are considered to be pests** as they feed on the sap of plants.

◀ Spittlebug nymphs produce 'cuckoo spit' by giving off a sticky liquid and blowing it into a frothy mass of white bubbles. As well as hiding the nymph from predators, these bubbles also protect the young bug from the drying effects of the sun.

Aphid

● **Aphids are related to cicadas.** They can be found in green, red or brown colours and are also known as greenflies.

● **They have a large abdomen** with two slender tubes called cornicles attached to it. The cornicles secrete wax.

● **Aphids with wings are weak fliers,** but they can cover great distances with the help of air currents.

● **Many aphids live underground** and suck sap from roots. Sometimes, they depend upon ants to carry them through tunnels in the soil and leave them out on fresh roots.

● **Aphids produce honeydew,** because they cannot digest all the plant sugar they eat. The honeydew is clear and sweet but it becomes black because a fungus grows on it.

● **Ants feed on the honeydew.** In return, the ants protect the aphids from their predators and even take them into their ant nests during bad weather.

● **Aphids breed in huge numbers.** An aphid can produce up to 100 young at a time.

● **Some aphids lay eggs** but some can reproduce without mating. These aphids give birth to live young .

● **Some aphids secrete strands of a waxlike substance** from their cornicles.

● **Aphids can cause damage to plants.** Their saliva causes plant leaves to fold and curl and even form galls.

◀ The cornicles are clearly visible on the abdomens of these aphids. The fluid they produce from these tubes may help to protect them from predators.

Mealybug

- **Mealybugs** are small insects up to 3 mm long and are found in huge clusters on leaves, twigs and tree bark. They are also called coccids.

- **Females do not usually have wings,** eyes or legs and remain immobile on plants. They are always covered in a white sticky coating of their own secretion. This protective coating looks like cornmeal.

- **Males do not have mouthparts.** However, they have wings and can fly.

- **Female mealybugs never lay their eggs in the open.** The eggs are attached to their bodies. However, some species of mealybugs can give birth to live young.

- **The flat, oval larvae crawl** about quite actively at first, but soon lose their legs and cover themselves with their mealy secretions.

- **A male mealybug's hind wings** are modified into tiny structures called halteres.

- **Mealybugs feed on the sap extracted from the plant tissues** and are considered to be pests of citrus trees and greenhouse plants.

- **Mealybugs can harm plants in many ways.** Galls can form on plants, or their stems can become twisted and deformed.

▲ Mealybug nymphs do not usually move after their first moult. They stay in one place, joined to plants only by their sucking mouthparts.

- **Mealybugs produce a sugary substance** known as honeydew. Ants often visit these insects for this sweet-tasting secretion.

- **Beetles, lacewings and caterpillars** prey on mealybugs.

◀ Male mealybugs usually have a pair of wings, well-developed legs and antennae and no mouthparts. Females are often wingless and legless, with reduced antennae.

Leafhopper

- **Leafhoppers** related to cicadas. They have a distinct leaflike shape and colour and are easy to recognize.

- **Leafhoppers can survive** in almost any part of the world. They are terrestrial bugs and can be found in deserts as well as in marshy and moist places.

- **Strong fliers,** leafhoppers are also capable of jumping considerable distances.

- **If these insects feed on plants,** they can cause the leaves to curl and affect the plant's growth.

▶ Leafhoppers are very common jumping insects that look rather like a narrow version of an adult spittlebug, or froghopper. They are tiny insects, only 2 to 15 mm long.

- **Leafhoppers are considered to be pests** and can cause damage to crops.

- **Leafhoppers search for their mates** by making special mating calls.

- **Females lay their eggs** in slits made in plant stems. The eggs can remain dormant for a month. In some species, the eggs can even remain dormant for a year.

- **Like aphids,** leafhoppers produce honeydew from the excess plant sap that they feed on.

- **These bugs communicate** with each other by producing low frequency sounds, which humans cannot hear.

- **Birds, reptiles and large insects,** such as wasps, are a threat to leafhoppers.

Stinkbug

- **Stinkbugs have glands** on their undersurface, from which they secrete a fluid. This fluid has a foul odour, which is why these insects are called stinkbugs.

◀ In some stinkbugs, the thorax extends down the back to form a protective shield, which almost covers the abdomen. These stinkbugs are also called shield bugs.

- **Their scent affects** many animals and protects the bug from predators.

- **Stinkbugs can be found in many colours,** such as green, grey, brown, red, black and yellow. They are one of the most notorious pests found in farmlands and orchards.

- **Some species of stinkbugs** produce a loud sound to defend themselves.

- **Stinkbugs have a compound** called glycerol in their blood. This prevents their blood from freezing in winter.

- **Many species of stinkbug** are active during the day, while others are nocturnal, especially the dark-coloured species, which live in thick grass or under leaves.

- **Stinkbugs normally feed on the sap from flowers,** leaves and fruits, which is why they destroy crops.

- **Male and female stinkbugs** are very similar in appearance, but the male is much smaller.

- **Stinkbug nymphs do not have wings** but adult stinkbugs are very good at flying.

★ STAR FACT ★
In some parts of Mexico, India and Africa, stinkbugs are relished as a source of food.

Water boatman

- **Water boatmen** are aquatic insects and are usually found in ponds and other freshwater bodies, such as canals and ditches.

- **Water boatmen have powerful, hairy legs** and are named after their habit of using their legs as oars to 'row' themselves through the water.

- **Most species of water boatman can fly,** but they often cling to water plants or live at the bottom of ponds.

- **Water boatmen do not have gills** and have to come to the surface to breathe.

- **Hairs on the body trap air bubbles.** This helps water boatmen to stay under water for long periods.

- **Water boatmen feed on algae,** plants and decaying animal matter.

- **Water boatmen find their food** on the bottom of ponds, canals and ditches, using their shovel-like front legs to scrabble it up.

▶ Water boatmen are not buoyant enough to float, so when they stop swimming, they sink to the bottom.

- **Some males rub their legs together** to make squeaky sounds that attract females.

- **The females lay their eggs under water.** The young nymphs that hatch from the eggs resemble adult water boatmen (without wings) but they moult five times before they become winged adults.

> ★ STAR FACT ★
> People in Mexico dry water boatmen eggs and eat them. In some countries, water boatmen are also sold as bird food.

Backswimmer

- **Backswimmers** spend almost their entire life floating in an upsidedown position in ponds. They use their legs like oars

- **These insects fly from one pond** to another in search of food.

- **While floating,** backswimmers identify direction with the help of light.

- **The underside** of backswimmers is dark in colour while the top of the body is light. The dark colour helps to hide the backswimmer from predators.

- **Backswimmers come to the water surface for air.** They carry a bubble of air under their belly, which helps them to stay underwater for a long time.

- **Backswimmers feed on other water insects,** worms and tadpoles.

◀ Backswimmers are shaped like boats, with a keel along their back. As they swim on their backs, the keel points downwards, like the keel on a boat. The bubble of air held beneath the body makes the insect float to the surface if it stops swimming.

- **Also known as the water bees,** the backswimmer's bite is painful. It can even bite humans.

- **Backswimmers look very similar** to water boatmen. However, water boatmen float the right way up and feed mainly on plants. Backswimmers, in contrast, are predators.

- **When attacking,** backswimmers inject toxins into their prey. This has a chemical reaction, which kills the prey.

- **Some species of backswimmers** are known to hibernate. During winter, these insects are found moving under the surface of frozen water.

Giant water bug

- **Giant water bugs** are like snorkellers. They have flaplike back legs to help them swim fast and special breathing tubes that resemble a snorkel.

- **By lying still in the water,** giant water bugs camouflage themselves so that they look like dead leaves.

- **These insects can fly** but they can survive only for about 15 minutes if they are taken out of water.

- **Giant water bugs hold their prey** with their claws and inject venom to paralyze it. Their mouthparts help them to pierce and suck fluid.

◄ Giant water bugs store air between their abdomen and their wings. To renew their air supply, they swim to the surface and extend a tube above the surface.

- **Giant water bugs are fierce hunters.** They feed on tadpoles, fish and insects.

- **Giant water bugs help to control** the mosquito population by feeding on mosquito larvae.

- **Males carry fertilized eggs on their backs** for about 10 days. They take care of the eggs until they hatch.

- **Giant water bugs are also known as 'toe biters'** because they may bite the toes of people wading.

- **In some Asian countries,** giant water bugs are considered a tasty snack.

> ★ STAR FACT ★
> Female giant water bugs lay their eggs on the backs of the males. They secrete a waterproof glue to stick the eggs onto the male's back.

Water strider

- **Water striders are often found** floating on still water and slow moving streams. They are one of the few insects that can survive in the sea and have even been found floating on the surface of the Pacific Ocean.

- **Water striders** (pond skaters) seldom go underwater. Their long legs help them to skate across the water.

- **These insects have six legs.** The front two are short and are mainly used to grasp prey.

- **Water striders have long, slender, hairy legs,** which end in a pad of water-repellent hairs so they do not break the surface of the water.

- **Some adults have wings,** while others are wingless.

- **Adults hibernate throughout winter** and mate in the spring.

> ★ STAR FACT ★
> Water striders are also known as Jesus bugs because of their ability to walk on water.

- **Water striders feed on insects** that fall into the water and aquatic insects that come to the surface to breathe.

- **Water striders communicate** by making vibrations and ripples on the water's surface.

- **Water striders move very quickly** and can run across water. If they were as big as humans, they would move as fast as a jet plane.

◄ The thin legs of a water strider help to spread its weight. The surface of the water bends into dips around the end of each leg, but does not break.

Cockroach

- **Cockroaches** belong to the order Blattodea of class Insecta. There are about 4000 known species of cockroaches. Some well-known cockroaches are oriental black beetles and croton bugs.

- **Cockroaches are found everywhere,** especially in bat caves, peoples' homes, under stones, in thick grass and on trees and plants. The cockroaches found in caves are usually blind.

- **These insects can be winged or wingless.** Adult cockroaches can be 1 to 9 cm long. They are nocturnal and prefer dark and damp places.

- **Cockroaches are swift creatures** and can run extremely fast. Their legs are adapted for quick movement. They have flat and oval bodies that help them to hide in narrow cracks in walls and floors.

- **Most cockroach species are omnivorous.** Their main food is plant sap, dead animals and vegetable matter but they will even eat shoe polish, glue, soap and ink.

- **Adults can live for up to two years.** Males and females are very similar in appearance but males have a pair of bristle-like styli.

★ STAR FACT ★
The name cockroach comes from the Spanish word cucaracha. These insects adapt quickly to changes in the environment and can even survive a nuclear explosion.

- **In some species,** females release pheromones or produce a hissing sound and wave their abdomen to attract male cockroaches.

- **Females can lay up to 30 to 40 eggs at a time** and can reproduce four times in a year. They store the eggs in a brownish egg case called an ootheca. The cockroach can either carry this egg case along with her or hide it somewhere. The young cockroaches are called nymphs.

- **Cockroaches play an important role** in balancing the environment by digesting a wide range of waste substances. They decompose forest and animal waste matter. At the same time, household cockroaches can contaminate food and spread diseases among humans.

▼ Cockroaches are not dirty creatures. They work hard to keep themselves clean in order to preserve a coating of wax and oils that prevents them from drying out. It is the bacteria they carry that makes them dangerous.

Madagascan hissing cockroach

- **Madagascan hissing cockroaches** are found on the island of Madagascar, off the south-east coast of Africa. They are large, wingless and famous for the hissing sound they make.

- **These cockroaches are chocolate brown,** with dark orange marks on their abdomen. Adults can grow to 10 cm in length.

- **A male cockroach** can distinguish between familiar males and strangers from the sound that they make.

- **Males look different from the females.** They have a large, hornlike structure behind their heads and hairy antennae.

- **These cockroaches feed on dead animal matter,** waste food or ripe fruits.

- **Females produce 30 to 60 eggs.** The eggs are stored in an egg sac. The eggs hatch into nymphs.

★ STAR FACT ★
Male hissing cockroaches are territorial. They fight by ramming and pushing with their horns and abdomens.

- **The nymphs of hissing cockroaches** moult six times before maturing into adult cockroaches. During moulting, the skin of a cockroach splits down the back and the cockroach wriggles out.

- **Newly moulted cockroaches** are whitish but their colour darkens within hours. Hissing cockroaches live for 2 to 5 years.

- **Madagascan hissing cockroaches** are easily bred.

◀ Hissing cockroaches hiss by pushing air thorugh breathing holes in their sides.

Oriental cockroach

- **Oriental cockroaches** are seasonal insects and can be most easily spotted during the spring and summer. They are found in places such as damp basements, drains, leaky pipes and kitchen sinks.

- **These cockroaches** are dark brown or black in colour so they are sometimes called 'black beetles'. Adults can grow up to 3.5 cm in length.

- **This cockroach is sometimes called** the 'shad roach' because its young appear in large numbers when shad (a fish) are swimming into fresh waters to breed.

- **Males have short wings** but females are wingless.

- **Females do have small wing stubs.** This is what makes them different from their nymphs.

- **A female can produce 5 to 10 egg cases** (oothecae) in her lifetime. Each egg case contains about ten eggs.

- **Young cockroach nymphs** hatch from the egg cases in 6 to 8 weeks and mature in 6 to 12 months. Adult cockroaches can live for up to one year.

◀ The head of this male oriental cockroach is almost hidden under the large hard collar (pronotum) at the front of the thorax. The cerci at the end of the abdomen are important sensory organs.

- **These cockroaches can enter homes** through sewer pipes, air ducts or any other opening.

- **Unlike other pest cockroaches,** oriental cockroaches do not have sticky pads on their feet and cannot climb slippery or smooth surfaces.

★ STAR FACT ★
Oriental cockroaches can survive for up to a month without food, if water is available.

Death's head cockroach

● **Death's head cockroaches** are large insects. They measure 5 to 8 cm in length. These cockroaches are mostly found in the Americas.

● **This cockroach is named after** the markings on its thorax, which look like skulls or vampires.

● **This insect is also known as** the palmetto bug or giant death's head cockroach.

● **Death's head cockroaches live mostly** in tropical forests or bat caves but they are also sometimes found in buildings.

● **Cockroaches are scavengers** and are active at night.

◀ *A fast runner, the death's head cockroach lives on the ground, searching through leaf litter or bat droppings for scraps of food.*

● **Death's head cockroaches are brownish in colour** with yellow and black marks on their body. While adults are beautifully coloured, the nymphs are dark in colour, although newly moulted nymphs are whitish.

● **The wings are very long** and cover their abdomen. The nymphs are wingless.

● **Females carry the eggs** inside their bodies and give birth to live young that hatch from the eggs.

● **Decaying plant and animal matter** are the favourite food of these cockroaches.

★ **STAR FACT** ★
Death's head cockroaches make good pets and are popular among cockroach lovers.

Crickets

● **Crickets belong to the order Orthoptera** and closely resemble grasshoppers. They are found nearly everywhere.

● **Crickets have flattened bodies,** long antennae and measure up to 5 cm. All crickets have wings.

● **These insects make sounds** that attract females and warn rival males to keep away.

● **Crickets produce these sounds** by rubbing the bases of their forewings.

● **Crickets feed on crops,** vegetables, plants, small animals, clothes and each other.

● **Some species of crickets** are considered to be pests because they can eat crops.

★ **STAR FACT** ★
The ancient Chinese conducted 'cricket matches' in which crickets would wrestle with each other.

▶ *All crickets have wings, but some cannot fly.*

● **Crickets are nocturnal** and have keen hearing and sight. Compound eyes help crickets see in many directions at once. Their hearing organs are found on their front legs.

● **Females have long ovipositors** to lay eggs. They carry the eggs until they find a safe place for the eggs to hatch.

● **In some parts of the world,** crickets are thought to be a sign of good luck.

Cave cricket

- **Cave crickets** are named after their habit of living in caves and other dark and damp places.

- **These crickets are also found in wells,** rotten logs, hollow trees and under damp leaves and stones.

- **These insects are also known as cave crickets** because they have a hump on their back.

- **Long hind legs** give cave crickets a spider-like appearance. They are good jumpers.

- **Cave crickets are brown in colour** and have long antennae. They do not have wings.

- **These insects cannot chirp or make sounds** because they are wingless. Crickets normally produce a high-pitched sound by rubbing their wings together.

- **Cave crickets are omnivorous** and feed on decaying organic matter, plants and vegetables.

- **In the spring,** females lay their eggs in soil. The nymphs and adults spend the winter in sheltered areas.

- **Cave crickets can damage articles** stored in boxes, garages and laundry rooms, as they love to live in cool and damp places.

- **Cave crickets are sometimes troublesome** in buildings and homes, especially in basements.

▼ *The long, sensitive antennae of the cave cricket help it to find its way around in the dark.*

Field cricket

- **Field crickets** are usually found in green fields and forested areas.

- **These insects are either black or brown** in colour and measure about 2.5 cm in length.

- **Spiky projections** called cerci are located on their abdomens.

- **Field crickets are omnivorous** and feed on plant seeds, smaller insects and fruits. Some species become cannibalistic if there is a shortage of food.

- **Males attract female crickets** by chirping and dancing. They perform a courtship dance before mating. The high-pitched sounds they make are heard from early spring to autumn.

- **Field crickets** are very active at night.

◄ *The antennae of the field cricket are longer than its body. It has shorter front wings than those of a grasshopper.*

- **Females usually lay** about 50 eggs at a time. They can lay up to 400 eggs in their lifetime.

- **Eggs are stored** in the female's ovipositor until she finds damp soil, where the eggs are deposited.

- **Field crickets do not usually survive the winter,** although their eggs can withstand harsh weather conditions.

- **Frogs, birds and other insects** feed on field crickets.

Katydid

- **Katydids** are usually green-coloured insects. They are 5 to 6 cm in length and have two pairs of wings.

- **These insects can be found** in grasslands, fields and rainforests.

- **The eardrums of katydids** are located on their front legs.

- **Katydids have long hind legs and antennae.** Their antennae help them search for food. Their long back legs help them to make powerful jumps.

- **Katydids can fly short distances** and feed on willow leaves, rosewood and citrus trees.

- **The males of various species** produce different sounds to communicate with members of their own species and with males of other species.

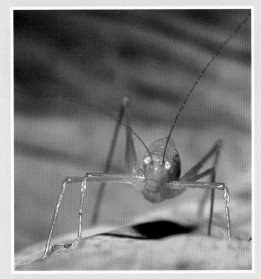

◀ *Katydids are well camouflaged as they rest among leaves during the day. Some tropical species even have fake leaf veins and chewed leaf edges to their wings to make them look even more like real leaves.*

- **Females respond to mating calls** by singing a soft 'song'.

- **The female lays her eggs in bark,** on twigs or on leaves. The eggs hatch into nymphs within three months. The total lifespan of katydids is about one year.

- **Katydids** are nocturnal.

★ **STAR FACT** ★
Katydids are named after their loud calls that sound like 'Katy-did-Katy-didn't'.

Grasshoppers

- **Grasshoppers are green or brown in colour.** Some species change colours in different seasons. They have six legs and a pair of compound eyes and wings.

- **Found almost everywhere,** grasshoppers prefer to live in green fields, meadows and forest areas.

- **There are three main types of grasshoppers** – long-horned, short-horned and pygmy.

- **Grasshoppers make a loud noise** during the mating season to attract a mate and scare rivals.

- **After mating,** the female lays eggs in low bushes or digs a hole in the soil to deposit eggs from her ovipositor.

- **Grasshoppers are herbivorous.** They feed on a variety of plants.

- **These insects are a threat to crops.** A large group of grasshoppers can destroy an entire crop.

★ **STAR FACT** ★
When captured, grasshoppers spit a brown liquid to protect themselves from their predators.

- **Flies, spiders, toads and reptiles** prey on grasshoppers and even eat their eggs.

- **In some parts of the world,** grasshoppers are considered a delicacy. They are ground into a meal, and sometimes fried or roasted and dipped in honey.

◀ *When a grasshopper is at rest, the wide, delicate, back wings are folded like a fan underneath the long, narrow front wings. The front wings are lifted up to allow the flying wings to spread out when the grasshopper flies.*

Bark bush cricket

- **Bark bush crickets** are so-called as they usually live on the bark of trees and shrubs in forests.

- **Bark bush crickets have flat bodies.** These insects are actually grasshoppers, and they are also known as long-horned grasshoppers.

- **These crickets are found in different colours** – from green to brown or even grey. They have underwings that are usually red and black in colour.

- **Bark bush crickets sing at night** and each species has a distinct song.

- **Bark bush crickets produce** a high-pitched chirping sound.

- **Unlike grasshoppers,** bark bush crickets produce sound by rubbing their forewings. Their ears are situated on their front legs.

- **Male bark bush crickets** are aggressive in nature and fiercely defend their territory.

- **The female lays her eggs** in the bark of trees and in leaf-stalks.

- **Sometimes, when the eggs are laid** in the tissue of living plants, they are transported to other countries with the plants.

- **Unlike grasshoppers,** females do not cover their eggs with an egg-pod (hard shell-like covering).

◀ Most species of bark bush cricket are omnivorous and feed on leaves, flowers, fruits and other insects.

Locust

- **Locusts** are found all over the world except in cold regions. They are dark brown in colour and their average length is 2.5 cm.

- **Locusts live in fields,** open woods or arid areas.

- **These insects are migratory** and can travel great distances. Locusts can be highly destructive of crops. A large swarm can consume 3000 tons of green plants in a single day.

- **Locusts can breed very quickly** compared to other insects. Some well-known species are the desert locust, the red-legged locust and the Carolina locust.

◀ Locusts can fly for up to 20 hours at a time.

- **Females lay their eggs** in soil. The nymphs are small and wingless. A female locust can lay 20 eggs at a time.

- **Locusts feed** on crops, weeds, grass or other plants.

- **Locusts have two phases.** In the solitary phase, locusts don't breed in large numbers. In the gregarious phase, the insect reproduces and grows quickly in the presence of an abundant food supply.

- **In the gregarious phase,** the locusts accumulate in large numbers. As a result, their habitat is not sufficient to support them, so they migrate in search of new feeding ground. This phenomenon is called swarming.

- **In some tribal groups,** dried locusts are eaten as food.

> ★ STAR FACT ★
> A locust swarm may occupy 26 to 777 sq km. Such swarms cast a shadow on the ground and appear like a huge black cloud.

Stick insect

● **Stick insects** belong to the order Phasmatodea. They look like leafless sticks and branches and are also called walkingsticks.

● **These insects are green or brown in colour** and spend their time clinging to trees, plants and shrubs.

● **Stick insects are excellent** at camouflaging themselves.

● **Some tropical species** of stick insect have spines on their legs, which blend with the thorns of plants. If threatened, they can stab their enemies. They also change their colour like chameleons.

● **Stick insects are active at night,** and feed on foliage.

● **Females are larger than the males.** Males can fly but the females can only glide.

● **Females produce pheromones to attract males.** They scatter their eggs randomly or hide them in order to protect them.

● **Asiatic stick insects** are the longest stick insects, measuring more than 30 cm.

● **Stick insects are the only insects** that can regenerate lost legs. If old limbs are cut off they can grow new ones.

▶ *If a stick insect is disturbed, it may suddenly drop to the ground or lose one of its legs to avoid capture. Many are wingless, but those with wings may flash their brightly coloured back wings to startle a predator.*

★ **STAR FACT** ★
Stick insects lie motionless and pretend to be dead to save themselves from their predators. This is called catalepsis.

Leaf insect

● **Leaf insects** belong to the order Phasmatodea and are most common in south-east Asia.

● **These insects have a unique appearance.** Their bodies are flat, irregular in shape and resemble a leaf. These insects are about 10 cm in length and sometimes have brown or yellow patches on their body.

● **Females are much larger** than males. They do not have hind wings and cannot fly but they have leaflike forewings.

● **The female can lay eggs** without mating with the male. This is called parthenogenesis.

● **A female scatters her eggs** on the ground. The eggs have a hard outer shell and resemble seeds, so predators do not feed on them.

★ **STAR FACT** ★
Leaf insects are leafy green in colour and are popularly known as walking leaves.

● **The eggs of the leaf insect** hatch in the spring.

● **Leaf insects are herbivorous,** feeding only on plant leaves.

● **Rodents, birds and other insects** feed on leaf insects.

● **Leaf insects are good at camouflage** and hiding from predators. They move very slowly and mimic the foliage on which they live.

◀ *This leaf insect would be very hard for predators to spot among green leaves, as long as it remained completely still.*

Damselfly

● **Damselflies** belong to the order Odonata and suborder Zygoptera. They have long, slender bodies and four long wings. They are weak fliers and timid predators.

● **These insects are the beautiful,** slender cousins of dragonflies but are not as ferocious. They have compound eyes and excellent eyesight.

● **Damselflies are usually found near water** and their nymphs live in the water until they mature into adults.

● **Mosquitoes, midgets, gnats and small water insects** are the preferred food of damselflies.

● **Damselfly nymphs have external gills** on the tip of their abdomen for breathing underwater. In dragonfly nymphs, these gills are internal.

● **Males and females mate during flight** or over shallow water. While mating, a male carries a female around to allow her to collect sperm from the front of his abdomen.

● **After mating,** females deposit their eggs in and around water.

● **The lifespan of a damselfly** is around one year but it can live up to two years.

● **During winter,** damselflies hibernate to survive the cold weather.

★ STAR FACT ★
Damselflies capture their prey with the help of their legs, folding them like a basket to form a trap. Once the insect is trapped it is transferred to the damselfly's mouth.

◄ The large compound eyes of a damselfly bulge out to the side. Damselflies also have long legs, which they use to hold insects captured in flight. Their legs are not suited to walking.

Dragonfly

> ★ STAR FACT ★
> Dragonflies can fly at 30 to 50 km/h.
> The design and mechanism of a helicopter
> was probably inspired by a dragonfly.

● **Dragonflies** are named for their fierce jaws, which they use for catching prey.

● **These insects can grow** up to 12 cm in length. They have long, slender bodies with two pairs of veined wings.

● **Larger dragonflies are called hawkers** while the smaller ones are called darters. Dragonflies have huge compound eyes, which cover their entire head.

● **Adult dragonflies survive on land** but their nymphs live underwater. They cannot survive harsh winters.

● **The lifespan of a dragonfly** ranges from six months to more than seven years.

● **Dragonflies mate** while they fly. The female dragonfly then deposits her eggs in water or inside water plants.

● **A female dragonfly** lays up to 100,000 eggs at a time. These eggs hatch into nymphs. These nymphs feed on fish, tadpoles and other small aquatic animals.

● **Dragonflies are beneficial to humans.** They prey on mosquitoes, flies and many small insects that are pests.

● **Experts have found dragonfly fossils** that are more than 300 million years old. These prehistoric dragonflies were as big as crows.

▶ *Each one of a dragonfly's wings can moves independently. This makes the dragonfly a very versatile flyer, able to hover, turn at 90 degree angles, dart backwards and forwards and come to a sudden stop.*

Praying mantis

● **Praying mantises** belong to the order Mantodea. These insects are closely related to cockroaches.

● **The praying mantis** is named for its posture. It holds its front legs together as if it were praying.

● **They can grow** up to 6.5 cm in length and have triangular heads that can turn in a full circle. They are generally green or brown in colour.

● **Praying mantises are camouflaged** as protection against predators. Their body colour blends with their environment. A species called the Asiatic rose mantis looks like flower petals.

● **Females are larger than the males.** They lay their eggs inside an egg case (ootheca) during the autumn.

● **Females secrete** a sticky substance to attach their eggs to plant stems. Nymphs hatch in the spring or summer.

◀ *A praying mantis moves its front legs rapidly to grab its prey. Sharp spines stop the prey from escaping.*

● **Praying mantises are carnivorous** and feed on insects. They can even attack small reptiles and birds, and can also become cannibalistic.

● **This insect silently stalks its prey** before attacking. While feeding, it holds its prey with its front legs.

● **Praying mantises are useful to humans.** They protect crops by feeding on pests. Sometimes farmers buy them for pest control. They are often kept as pets, even though large praying mantises can hurt people.

> ★ STAR FACT ★
> A female praying mantis often eats the male
> while mating!

Antlion

- **Antlions** are named after the larva's habit of feeding on ants and other insects. Adult antlions feed on pollen or nectar or do not feed at all.

- **Antlions resemble dragonflies.** They both have long slender bodies and four delicate wings. However, unlike dragonflies, antlions are nocturnal in nature.

- **These insects are found in damp areas** where vegetation is thick. Antlions are also found near riverbeds.

- **Some antlion larvae** make a pit in the sand by moving around in a spiral path and throwing out sand.

- **While making the pit,** the larva leaves behind squiggly doodles on the sand. For this reason, antlions are also known as doodlebugs.

▼ The stout, clubbed antennae of adult antlions are very different from the short, thin antennae of dragonflies.

▲ An antlion larva waits at the bottom of its pit trap for an unsuspecting insect to fall down into its pincer-like jaws.

- **The larva then waits inside the pit** and feeds on insects that fall into it. When the prey struggles to escape, the larva throws sand on it to make it fall back down into the pit.

- **Once the larva has sucked the body juices** of its victim, the remains of the insect are thrown out of the pit. These larvae are voracious eaters and can eat even adult antlions when food is scarce.

- **An antlion larva** secretes silk and pupates inside a cocoon made of soil and silk.

- **Unlike the larva of other insects,** an antlion larva secretes silk from the tip of its abdomen instead of its mouth.

★ STAR FACT ★
Antlion larvae have a peculiar appearance. Their shape has inspired the creation of monsters in many Hollywood science fiction movies.

Mantisfly

- **Mantisflies** are named after their folded pair of front legs, which look like those of praying mantises. Although these insects look similar, they are not related.

- **These insects are not common** and are found in tropical regions.

- **Mantisflies, along with lacewings and antlions,** belong to the order Neuroptera.

- **Mantisflies lay their rose-coloured eggs** on slender plant stalks.

- **The mantisfly has a complicated development cycle.** It has two growth stages as a larva and two more stages as a pupa.

◀ A mantisfly grabs its prey with its huge front legs. The wings of a mantisfly are very different from those of a praying mantis.

- **The larva of one species of mantisfly** is a parasite of wolf spiders. A larva enters a cocoon and preys upon the egg or young. The larva pierces the egg or spider with its pointed mouthparts and feeds on it.

- **The larva then pupates** inside the spider's cocoon.

- **The parent spider** watches over the cocoon, unaware of the presence of the parasite mantisfly.

- **Some mantisflies** mimic wasps and bees for protection.

- **Mantisflies are as predatory** as praying mantises and have similar feeding habits.

Lacewing

- **Lacewings** are delicate green or brown insects, which are named after their thin, translucent, lacelike wings.

- **These insects have long,** threadlike antennae and their eyes are bright golden yellow or brown in colour.

- **Birds and other predators** avoid lacewings because they give off a pungent odour similar to garlic.

- **Lacewings are not good fliers** because their wings are too weak to support their weight for long distances.

- **A lacewing lays a large number of eggs** at a time. The eggs are white and are glued to a twig or leaf.

- **Lacewing larvae feed on small insects.** They eat a lot of aphids (greenfly) in a day and are sometimes used to control the population of aphids in crop fields.

- **The larvae of lacewings** are sometimes reared commercially to get rid of pests. Apart from aphids, these larvae feed mealybugs, leafhoppers, caterpillars, moths and other insects.

- **Lacewing larvae have 'jaws',** which they use to suck the body fluids of the prey after injecting it with paralyzing venom.

- **Many species of adult lacewings** do not eat other insects. Instead, they feed on nectar, pollen and honeydew.

- **Some lacewing larvae** build camouflage from debris, including the skin and other remains of their prey.

◀ A lacewing has two pairs of wings. When it rests, it holds its wings together like a roof over its body.

Stonefly

● **Stoneflies** are an ancient order of insects which has been around for nearly 300 million years.

● **Stonefly nymphs** cling to stones in clear mountain streams or lakes. They are eaten by fish and are also used as models for artificial fish bait.

● **Some stonefly nymphs** breathe through gills near their legs. Others obtain oxygen through their body surface

● **Adult stoneflies** live on land. However, they never wander too far from water, and spend their time crawling over stones. Stoneflies live for two to three years.

● **Female stoneflies deposit their eggs** in deep water. To prevent the eggs from floating away, they attach them to rocks with a sticky secretion.

● **A stonefly nymph resembles an adult** but does not have wings and its reproductive organs are not as well developed.

● **Fishes often attack** female stoneflies when they try to deposit their eggs in streams.

▶ *The flat body of a stonefly nymph helps to stop it being washed away as it clings to stones at the bottom of streams.*

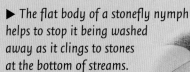

● **Stonefly nymphs feed** on underwater plants. Some species are carnivorous and feed on aquatic insects. Most adults feed on algae and pollen.

● **Stoneflies are sensitive to water pollution.** Experts use these insects to study the level of water purity.

> ★ STAR FACT ★
> Some male stoneflies attract females by drumming their abdomen against a hard surface. They are popularly known as 'primitive drummers' for this reason.

Scorpionfly

● **Scorpionflies** are a small group of insects with dark spots on their two pairs of membranous wings. These primitive insects have been around for 250 million years.

● **The rear body part** of some males is curled upwards, similar to a scorpion's. Only males resemble scorpions.

● **Adult scorpionflies have modified mouthparts.** They have a long beak pointing downwards.

● **Scorpionflies feed** on live as well as dead insects. Some also feed on pollen, nectar and plants.

● **They are predators** and often steal their food from spiders' webs. Scorpionflies catch their prey with their hind legs.

● **While mating,** a male scorpionfly secretes a sweet, sticky secretion, on which the female scorpionfly feeds.

> ★ STAR FACT ★
> During the mating season, a male scorpionfly offers the female a gift. This courtship gift can be a dead insect or a drop of his saliva.

● **A female scorpionfly lays her eggs** in wooden crevices and soil. The eggs hatch and the larvae live and pupate in loose soil or waste material.

● **Scorpionfly larvae** feed on dead and rotten plant and animal matter. Some larvae also feed on small insects.

● **Scorpionflies are considered** helpful because they keep the environment clean by feeding on dead insects.

◀ *The most distinctive feature of scorpionflies is their elongated head with a long 'beak', which ends in biting jaws.*

Silverfish

- **The silverfish** is a primitive insect, which belongs to the order Thysanura.

- **These insects** are soft-bodied and do not have wings. Silverfish have a longish body with three tail filaments.

- **Silverfish are silver or brown** and move very swiftly.

- **Silverfish prefer to live** in dark, humid places. They are mostly found in moist, warm places, such as kitchens and baths.

- **These insects feed on flour,** glue, paper, leftover food and even clothes. Silverfish can easily survive for months without food.

- **Silverfish can destroy books** and are considered to be indoor pests.

- **Silverfish mate** in a unique way. A male spins a silk thread and deposits his sperm on it. The female then picks up the sperm and uses it to fertilize her eggs.

- **A female silverfish can lay** up to 100 eggs in her lifetime. After mating, she deposits clusters of her eggs in cracks or crevices.

- **Even after maturing into adults,** these insects continue to moult. They can live for two to eight years.

- **Silverfish are generally harmless to humans,** but they can contaminate food.

◀ *Silverfish are named after the shiny scales that cover their carrot-shaped body (bottom right). They belong to a group of insects called bristletails because their abdomen ends in a bristly tail.*

Springtail

- **Springtails** belong to the order Collembola.

- **Springtails are wingless insects** measuring up to 5 mm in length. Unlike most other insects, springtails do not have compound eyes.

- **These insects have a springlike organ,** known as a furcula, under their abdomen. It helps them to leap high into the air.

- **Springtails do not have a respiratory system.** They breathe through their cuticle (hard skin).

- **Even though springtails can jump,** they normally crawl from one place to another.

- **Decaying vegetable matter,** pollen, algae and other plants are the preferred food of springtails.

- **Springtails prefer to live in soil** and moist habitats. However they can survive almost anywhere in the world including Antarctica and Arctic regions.

- **A female springtail lays** approximately 90 to 150 eggs in her lifetime.

- **The lifespan of a springtail** is one year or less.

▼ *Springtails live in moist places because their bodies dry out easily. They are usually a grey or brown colour, sometimes with mottled colours for camouflage.*

★ **STAR FACT** ★
Springtails are also called snow fleas as they can survive in extreme cold. They are active even in freezing weather.

INDEX